SO~~

Daryl L. Meyers

Copyright © 2023
All Rights Reserved
ISBN: 978-1-916787-42-1

All rights reserved. No part of this publication may be reproduced, distributed, or transmitted in any form or by any means, including photocopying, recording, or other electronic or mechanical methods, without the author's prior written permission, except in the case of brief quotations embodied in critical reviews and certain other non-commercial uses permitted by copyright law. For permission requests, please get in touch with the author.

Regarding the manuscript: *"it is an incredibly inspiring and thought-provoking work. The author's ability to weave together spiritual and philosophical ideas with personal reflections is truly remarkable, and we believe readers of all backgrounds will find something meaningful in his words.*

The theme of evolution, of creation, constantly unfolding and expanding, is one that resonates deeply throughout the book. The author's writing evokes a sense of wonder and awe at the vastness and complexity of the universe, and it is clear that he has a deep reverence for the natural world and its rhythms.

We particularly appreciated the way he has approached spirituality and religion in his essays. His words are inclusive and welcoming, recognizing that each person's journey is unique and valid. He offers guidance and support without prescribing a specific path or doctrine, allowing readers to find their own way."

Amazon Publishing Team

Daryl's deep sense of spirituality and oneness is evident in his essays and reflections. This compilation is a brilliant collection of positive, inspiring messages of hope, understanding and encouragement. Each piece speaks both independently and to every audience offering inspiration and clarity. This is a book I will refer to over and over again.

Julie Ramsey

Contents

Dedication i
Acknowledgments ii
About the Author v
Foreword 1
Introduction 3
Open My Eyes 4
Be Still and Know 5
The Sound of Music 7
Facing Life – Moving On 9
Distracted 11
What Time Is It? 13
Never Forgotten 16
From The External to the Internal 17
On The Other Side of Reason 19
The Child Within 21
You Own What? 23
The Gift 26
Who Am I? 27
Concepts For Living 30
A Force of Nature 32
As The Years Go By 36
Beauty or the Beast 38
Now You See Him – Now You Don't 40
The "Present" 50
Who Says I Have to Be Right 51
A Celebration in Time 53
Everyday Heroes 55

Being A Part of the Team 57
To Be or Not to Be 58
The Me That I Am 59
And The Truth Shall Make You Free 61
Darkness May Come, But So Does the Dawn 63
The Road to Success 64
Common Ground 66
Face to Face 74
Life is For-giving, Not For-getting 76
If Only 79
Treasures in Time 80
So How Do We Measure Up? 82
In Search of Innocence 85
The Silent Treatment 87
Detours 90
Possibilities Unlimited 91
On Becoming a Child 93
A Journey Through Time 95
A Word to The Wise 96
The Journey 99
Accepting the Unacceptable 101
The Awakening 102
Hope 104
The Spirit of Who We Are 106
Commitment 108
The Shadow Side of the Beautiful 109
Standing Together 110
It's Friday! 111
Love 113

Time Out	114
Seeing is Believing, Or Is It?	115
Life Without Limits	117
Happiness is …	118
Imperfectly Perfect	120
Another Look at Love	125
The Challenge of Change	126
The Ideal and the Real	127
Out of the Silence	135
A Composition of the Ages	137
Reflections or Reality	139
Your Attention Please	141
Returning Home	143
The Best Gifts in Life Are Free	149
Ageless Solutions For A Better Tomorrow	150
What in the World's Going On?	155
Special Section	164
Christmas – A Time to Remember	165
Holiday Memories	167
The Spirit of the Season	170
Christmas – A Time for Embracing The "Present"	172
To Broadway With Love	174
A New Beginning	176
A Cry of Innocence	178
Reflections	182
References	217

Dedication

To those who seek strength and direction in a world of conflict and confusion. To the homeless and forgotten; the abused and forsaken who struggle just to survive. To all who pray for the dawn of a new day This book is dedicated to you for you are the ones to change the world.

Acknowledgments

"No man is an island; no man stands alone."

- **John Donne**

No matter how gifted in music, in writing or the arts, none of us can claim independence from the influence and the assistance of others, past or present, nor is the author of this book an exception. All talents and abilities passed on through heredity, cultural or educational advantage, are but gifts to be shared. Whether recognized or not, without those who contributed to this book, it would be no more than an idea.

It has been said that it takes a village to raise a child. Perhaps this is also true in bringing a project from concept to reality. Given the author's limited ability in technology and the world of social media, he could not have asked for a better team.

As a friend of many years and former consultant, Julie Ramsey's creative abilities are well known to the author. Her background in all aspects of this project including her experience in working with social media, editing, website setup and design, as well as her ability to coordinate it all is beyond amazing. Her son, Nick Ramsey's expertise as a specialist in information technology (Factotum IT), has also been very helpful not only in setting up the website but in other technical aspects of this project.

Kirk Hutchinson, owner of Daystar Recording Studios, whom the author has worked with in music for over 30 years, not only has one of the best studios in Colorado but is also one of the finest musicians and composers anywhere. His formal and informal education qualify him as a software engineer as well as in music

Over many years the author has also had the opportunity of listening to lectures and group discussions led by Dr. Leland Kaiser, a nationally known consultant in healthcare. Even though he is no longer with us, his knowledge and wisdom into issues involving some of the deeper insights and concepts regarding the human experience has without doubt had a significant influence on the author and many of the thoughts presented in this book.

Another very important member of the team in more ways than one is the author's wife, Kerstin. Her assistance has especially been helpful in editing essays and other materials for this book. Although originally from Sweden, her ability in English is often better than her husband's. She still outdoes him in Scrabble ... about nine games to one. Given that creative people are not always the easiest to live with, her patience with the author – that's me - and the many years it has taken to get this project together are worth more than one medal of honor.

Years ago the author and his wife went on an unexpected trip to Poland which eventually turned into a 20-year opportunity of getting acquainted with a wonderful Polish family - the Rymszas. They have had much more of an influence on the author and his wife than they might realize. Agnieszka, the youngest daughter, has even contributed some of her photography to this book as well as to the website. Although different today, along with the support of her husband. Tomek, she was the major contributor to the original website layout and design.

On another trip and another "chance meeting," additional support was provided by Brittany Gerhardt who lives in Canada. Though a teenager at the time, she did an excellent job in typing out some of the hand-written notes for this project. Thanks Brittany. You are a definite reminder to never underestimate what a teenager can do!

Many other hands have also been involved in this project, including a person from years ago, Susan Dyer, who aware or not, encouraged the creative writing skills of the author. And there are others as well, too many to name, and many whose names may have slipped from memory, but their contribution to this project named or not is just as important.

Above all recognition must go to the One who not only creates but brings beauty and inspiration to the life experience along paths and through channels often unexpected. If this book can be a channel of light in a time of darkness to even a few, it will have served its purpose.

About the Author

Born and raised in Atlanta, Georgia, Daryl attended college at Southern Adventist University near Chattanooga, Tennessee. He later graduated with master's and doctorate degrees from Andrews University in Berrien Springs, Michigan. He also studied abroad at a private college in England, where he met a young lady from Sweden whom he later married.

Their greatest joy is their family, two sons, a daughter-in-law, and two grandsons. They also enjoy outdoor activities especially race walking and power walking.

Besides his college and university studies, Mr. Meyers has had experience in writing, music, and public speaking, which he has continued to develop over the years. He has shared his love of music in the U.S., Europe, and Africa.

While working in Africa he had opportunities to write articles for national magazines in both England and the U.S., including interviews with a former President of Liberia, William R. Tolbert, and Shirley Temple Black, former child movie star and U.S. Ambassador to Ghana.

Mr. Meyers has also been involved in health care for many years, supporting patients and their families as hospital chaplain and community relations director. He also served the City of Brighton for 10 years as a councilman.

Through his music and writing, Mr. Meyers's desire is to support and encourage people across all backgrounds to make decisions that will bring meaning and joy to their journey on this adventure we all share together called life.

Foreword

The following essays address many of the issues and challenges common to us all and are not so much a guide to be followed as they are a reflection of the author's personal journey as well as much he still has to learn. They were written over a period of many years under different circumstances with no particular theological or cultural perspective in mind and are meant to support people everywhere of all backgrounds. Though expressed in different ways, the reader will find certain themes emphasized or repeated such as the importance of time apart (becoming more centered) and the close relationship there is and interdependence that exists throughout all creation.

The music on the author's website, both original and selected, has been chosen to compliment the essays with lyrics that address the experiences we all go through; love and loss, joy, sorrow, success and failure.

Although times have changed, it is apparent we have not. We speak proudly of the human family and how important our relationships, yet our actions betray us. We still believe we are separate from one another, that we can live however we want, treat anyone the way we wish without it affecting our world or the world around us. We have yet to understand how this illusion affects every aspect of our lives. We long for peace and prosperity but have created anything but.

It would seem we have forgotten a universal truth, a theme that runs throughout many of these essays, that nothing is separate from anything and never has been. Unfortunately, we have put leaders in positions of authority, many of whom have forgotten this truth and are out of touch with the deeper issues of the human experience. Many of these leaders no longer see the welfare of the majority as a priority and have allowed greed, power and control to dominate their thinking and influence their decisions.

We have now come to a place in human history more critical than we have ever known, for the decisions we make or allow to be made will determine not only our future, but that of our children and generations to come. If we continue to let our imaginations separate us and act accordingly, the future of the human race will be extremely limited, if at all.

Though this book of essays does not in any way cover the entire range of human feelings and emotions, nor will everyone agree with what the author has written, perhaps there are some thoughts presented readers can relate to. Above all if the essays remind us of how much we share in common, then this book will have accomplished something of value.

Introduction

In a world where sadness and sorrow are the daily companions of many, where competition has taken the place of compassion and power the place of peace. In a world where courage gives way to fear, and greed is blind to need, we must continue to believe, to hope that someday there will be a new tomorrow, that someday soon we will see the dawn of a new day, a new world in which the rights of all are respected and the potential of all encouraged.

Open My Eyes

Open my eyes that I might see,

Beyond the now to eternity.

Open my ears that I might hear,

Music beyond the atmosphere.

Open my heart that I might feel,

the joy of knowing that You are near.

Be Still and Know

In a world where drive and financial worth define success, living with integrity, where personal values are the driving force, is rarely encouraged, much less accepted.

Paths that could lead to more meaningful experiences are often obscured by directives from our minds or discounted by the mixed messages of our society. Many feel disconnected from themselves, from others, and from almost everything else. Life is no longer lived but endured, a walk through the shadows in a world of struggle along paths that seem to go nowhere.

The desire to be understood, to feel secure in a world that seems obsessed with the superficial and undermines the human spirit, causes many to move in directions under normal circumstances they would not choose, with less than satisfactory results.

Given the intense schedules common to most of us, we tend to push aside personal needs, plunge into the activities of the day and then wonder why we feel so worn out, so dissatisfied when the day comes to an end. We sense something is missing, something is wrong, but we can't quite figure out what.

Although we do our best, at times, we feel lost, subject to the whims of fate or whatever it is that awaits our destiny.

We wander through our days wondering what it's all about and if we will ever get to our destination, wherever that is.

Could it be the answer that best meets our needs is simpler than we think? Is it possible the way we treat life has much to do with how life treats us? Could it be how we begin our day has more of an influence on how it ends than we realize?

If, before we move into our daily routine, we were to restructure our days, allowing time at its beginning to become more centered, more present, our journeys throughout the day might be different and less stressful. The barriers our minds have put in place might finally give way to new ways of thinking, new ways of exploring opportunities and addressing challenges.

When we take time apart in the silence, as if awakening from a dream, we begin to see things as they really are. The artificial and transitory give way to the real. Limitations imposed give way to opportunities and adventures of which we were unaware. Suddenly life looks different. In the stillness, our ability to see what is most important becomes clearer. Limited horizons begin to fade, and new possibilities open before us.

❧ *The door to wisdom opens when the mind is quiet, the body still, and the soul is allowed to speak.*

The Sound of Music

Very few of us are gifted musicians, but we are all musical. It's in our genes. It's who we are. It's as natural as a sunrise and as profoundly simple as a baby's smile.

All around us and within is a symphony of sounds more magnificent than any orchestra, past or present. Melodies full of beauty and joy are constantly being created.

In the gentle fragrance of a flower. The laughter of a child. The cry of a newborn. In the feel of freshness at the dawn of a new day. In the drone of a hundred frogs in chorus on a dark rainy night or the whisper of eagles' wings in flight to the unknown.

It can be heard in the natural rhythm of sound and shadows within the silence of an enchanted forest, in the magic and charm of a diamond-studded sky on a cold winter's night, in the dance of the wind, or the echo of a canyon. It can be heard in the rush of a river or the steady drumbeat of a million waves on a thousand shores.

In and through them all is music both natural and more beautiful than any composition ever created, and you and I are part of it all.

Can you hear it? Do you feel it? It's as close as your next breath, your next heartbeat and as real as the earth beneath your feet. Listen closely, for its melodies will touch and change your life.

Who knows what songs are possible when the human heart beats in harmony with the Divine. Who knows what beauty lies in the making when the soul is allowed to sing.

🕊 *Like love, beauty cannot be defined, only experienced.*

Facing Life – Moving On

Having an advanced education with an income to match is absolutely essential to experience the "good life" in our society, or so we are told. But reality suggests these messages are incorrect and incomplete, that there is more to a life well lived than we realize and far more than our traditions and cultures allow.

As the moments fade into days and months to years, circumstances change. Life is like a kaleidoscope of colors and feelings, of experiences that are continually changing. New designs suddenly appear, merging into the unexpected, life creating life, the natural recreating itself into patterns of beauty, unparalleled, unseen, unknown until now.

Conditions and climates are never the same. They will never be just the way we want them to be, nor will people always think or act the way we feel they should. At times illness will knock at our door, and we may have to answer. Life comes to us the way it comes, but it always has something to give us if our hearts and minds are open to its whisperings. What we do with these gifts is up to us.

To try and avoid the unpleasant may not be best. As with athletes, it's the struggle and strain that builds strength and endurance. Our personal growth is determined more by how we face hard times than the results of anything we inherit.

Compliments are welcome and sometimes needed, but often it's the more demanding, strenuous experiences that help us grow.

The terrain ahead may be rugged. Chances are we're going to get bounced around a bit. But with patience and perseverance, a mind willing to receive, and a heart that's open to the unexpected, we will make it, and we just might be surprised at how much we've grown in the process.

Life seldom comes to us as we desire or expect.
It comes in ways often unexpected or unacceptable but when allowed has the power to transform.

Distracted

None of us come into the world empty-handed. Though unrealized or suppressed because of feelings of inadequacy, all of us have abilities that can make a difference in the lives of others. Though we may think otherwise, our journey in this world has nothing to do with climbing the ladder of success, making a name for ourselves, or achieving financial worth, but rather a willingness to become channels through which the gifts we've been given can encourage those struggling to exist, much less live.

Unfortunately, few of us are left to follow our dreams or develop the abilities we've been given without outside influences trying to get us off course. Well-meaning friends and multimedia sources encourage decisions, not always in our best interest. We are surrounded by strong personalities who attempt to manage our lives and turn us from our truth to theirs.

Though it is true interruptions can break up a routine and free us from certain patterns of behavior, they can also move us in directions that do not reflect our strengths or the overall plan for our lives.

How easy it is to get distracted. Our minds begin to wander with actions close behind. Before we know it, we're on a side road that's going nowhere fast. Our attention is now on 101 little things which have little meaning rather than what's most important. Because our minds have gotten us off track, we end up contributing less to life than we could.

To move in the direction which is consistent with the creative abilities and talents we've been given takes courage, especially when others disagree, but if we press on, we can become channels of light, turning the darkest night for someone into day. No, we may never have our name in lights, but we can be a light for others if we so choose.

> *When we see things as they really are, we will know everything is meant to bring us exactly what we need.*

What Time Is It?

What would it be like if there were no clocks, no mirrors, no way of measuring time? If life just flowed on and on, and there were no sunsets, no beginnings, no endings, just one continuous moment of now? How would that affect the way we live?

In a timeless, mirrorless world, a world with no means of measurement, nothing would be the same. Old and young, attractive or not, past and future would be seen in an entirely new light, that is if they could be seen at all.

Could it be that what we think is constant is not; that time is relative, that it changes according to the experiences we go through, that sometimes forever is but a few moments (time stands still) and a few moments like forever? When life comes in ways unexpected causing pain or loss, the days drag by. There seems to be no end in sight. At other times … time flies. The years go by faster than the speed of light.

Is it possible time is more an illusion than a reality, something we've made up? The truth is the only time we have is now. Is the turtle concerned about tomorrow or the possum about the past? Does the kangaroo need a calendar? Ask a tree, or a flower what time it is and they'll wonder what you're talking about. Ask a squirrel or a robin the time of day, and they would have no idea how to respond. To them, time does not exist. Their only consciousness is the present. In a sense, timelessness defines all creation.

Everything is evolving and changing, all of it happening in the present, in each moment of now.

Although our minds take us on journeys into the past or project us into the future, we cannot live, work, or play in any other dimension than the present. The fragrance of a flower, the beauty of a sunset, the aroma of freshly baked bread coming from the kitchen can only be experienced in the present.

In the world of nature, there are no savings accounts, insurance, or retirement plans. All of life is lived from moment to moment. Although we try, it's impossible to live any other place but in the present. In a sense, the past and future do not exist except in our minds. "And time shall be no more," the words of ancient wisdom, just might have more meaning than we realize.

The only dimension that is real is the present. It's in the eternal moment of now that we are born, live, and die. Within each moment, the mysterious and magical create mosaics of possibilities beyond our imagination. Here is where, according to our choices, opportunities are provided that give direction to our lives.

We are like children given the present in which to play, and what a "present" it is. Whether we choose hide-and-seek, tag, or make-believe makes no difference as long as we don't hurt one another.

Of course, we can't play our games forever. Eventually, a quiet voice speaks to our hearts. "All right children. No more games. This moment is almost over. It's time for you to come home; it's your children's turn to go out and play."

And so, much more quickly than we realize, this adventure we call life comes to an end. To enjoy the journey and all the games we've made up can be a great experience if we learn to play fairly and to live totally and completely in the present, for the truth is, there is …

No **O**ther **W**ay

Sometimes we must step back in order to move forward; slow down in order to catch up, stand still in order to make progress.

Never Forgotten

No matter how obscure, no life is unknown to the great Creator of all.

Flowers scattered in wild arrays of beauty in a thousand forests across a million fields are never lost to the hand that has made them.

Every cloud in every sky, every drop in every wave that crashes along the shores of time are known to him.

No leaf falls to the ground without his notice. There is neither a time nor place when he is not present.

Each face, no matter what the race, is held sacred, close to the heart of Infinite Love.

No one is ever forgotten. All are part of a divine plan that reaches beyond the temporary to the eternal.

From The External to the Internal

Beauty may only be "skin deep," but it definitely plays an important role in our world today. Shapes and forms, fads, and fashions are all part of the cultural mindset of our society.

"To look good" whatever the cost, is a priority to many.

Unfortunately, or fortunately, none of us were consulted by mother nature when bodies were being assigned. We got what heredity gave us. For some, this was okay. For others, a little better than okay. To the greater majority of us however, mother nature was very creative. She made us extremely "normal."

We come in all shapes, colors, sizes, and conditions. Some of us are tall, skinny, and a bit wiry; others are short and fluffy. Some are petite, cuddly, and cute; others a bit out of proportion, a little clumsy even.

Some are pretty "hairy;" and others leave "nothing" to the imagination. We are the sum total of our parts and more. We are special. We are people. We are human.

Could it be, at times, we are centered more on how we look than we should? Are we no more than shapes and bodies that move? Could it be there are other things of value beyond appearance, that maybe, just maybe, our sense of self and of others is a bit distorted?

Regardless of what we look like on the outside, life is special, and so are we.

Each of us has something of value to offer. Perhaps we need to look a little closer, a little deeper. Like gold, beauty is rarely found on the surface. It's the effort, the process it takes to bring it from the earth and refine it, that makes it of value.

So, let's take another look. If what we "see" about ourselves and others is a bit out of focus, it might be time for another eye exam.

On The Other Side of Reason

Across the centuries in almost every culture, logic and reason have held a place of honor in human affairs. If it's reasonable, it's acceptable. To move beyond the known to the unknown is a risk very few have been willing to take, but as history has proven, progress, though slow, has only come about by those who have challenged the norm, risked ridicule, and even life itself in order to bring new truths and concepts into being.

Whether in science, theology, or psychology, progress is extremely limited if reason alone has the final word. To disallow the new in order to hold on to the old is comfortable but never progressive.

Could it be that our understanding of life is more limited than we think? Is it possible that our measurements of ourselves and of that which lies beyond are inaccurate or irrelevant?

When life moves in a direction unexpected, contrary to our beliefs or the values of our society, we feel disoriented, out of balance, lost. Things appear upside down when it could be the unexpected or unwelcome are actually turning things "right side up."

Though we may resist, life often makes itself known to us in ways outside and contradictory to our social norms or theological mandates, at times shattering our most sacred concepts. It may speak to us in the darkness as well as the light; through the distorted or discounted, the rejected, the unclean, or the unworthy.

It may appear to us in ways unexpected or unacceptable, opening up vistas of the eternal that go far beyond anything our present world construct allows. If we are conscious and accepting of His presence, the darkest night will turn into a brilliance more awesome than the sun on a clear summer day.

To recognize our limitations and be open to the unknown puts us on a course that will expand our horizons and move us toward dimensions of insight and understanding far beyond anything we could ever imagine.

The Child Within

To a child, life is exciting, a gift to be celebrated, an adventure just begun. The world's a playground waiting to be explored. There's so much to do, so much to see, and nothing is beyond reach. Today is all there is. Tomorrow doesn't exist.

But time and change are beyond our control. The years go by. The child becomes an adult. Things are different now. Life is no longer the adventure it once was. One must struggle to achieve, fight to succeed. Life is serious business. Play is now a temporary escape from the harsh realities of a world to be conquered.

What happened? What went wrong? Did we miss a turn somewhere on the way to adulthood? Must growing up mean leaving behind the magical, adventuresome spirit of childhood? When we entered this world, there were tears, and when we leave, if we aren't allowed to play, there will be tears again.

Maybe it's time we took a second look at where we're headed. Perhaps we need to go back, revisit those early years and reclaim the childlike trust and innocence we knew so well when we were young.

Could it be that somewhere along the way, our priorities have gotten a bit mixed up? Is it possible there is more to life than climbing the ladder of success, getting to the top, and having it all? That maybe, just maybe, the simple things in life are still of most value? Could it be the playfulness, simple and carefree spirit of a child is still worth considering even for adults? Could it be?

> 🕊 *As a glorious sunrise, beauty like love is natural. If allowed, it flows in, around and through us.*

You Own What?

There is a secret known throughout the world of nature but, as of yet, not fully understood by humans. Nothing in this world is owned. We are but caretakers, stewards of that which is. No matter what we are born with or acquire over time, be it fame, fortune, good looks, or educational advantage, eventually we will leave it all behind.

Many have tried to hold on to whatever they felt was theirs, but none have succeeded. Though superior in many ways to other life forms, we are the only species on the planet who accept and live the illusion of ownership. For those among the lower order of creation, it is understood that everything is provided, but nothing is owned. The boundaries we build to protect our homes, our monuments, and grand cathedrals mean nothing to them, nor are our cries of desecration, for in their world there are no limits or restrictions. The world is theirs and they know it.

Although of value far beyond our ability to comprehend, the physical universe is temporary and continually changing, a created reality locked into the limitations and boundaries of time whereas the creative source, the energy, the spirit, and intelligence behind the universe is forever, eternal, never-ending.

Like other life forms, when we came into the world, we brought nothing with us but a spirit of adventure. The whole world lay at our feet, just waiting to be explored. We had no idea about our heritage, how humble or well-to-do our circumstances, or how elaborate or tastefully decorated our homes. All we knew was we had arrived. We were here in a universe of universes on a planet called Earth, about to explore and celebrate the wonders of an experience called life.

Everything we touched and everything we saw was amazing. To us, the world was a place beyond description, both mysterious and magnificent. We embraced and celebrated it all, for though we could hold on to nothing like the rest of creation, we somehow knew everything was ours. Our inheritance, the world we were born into, was far beyond anything we could ever have imagined.

Unfortunately for most, over the years struggle and the desire for more gradually replaced the truth we knew as children, that no matter who we were or how challenging the way everything needed for our lives had already been provided.

The truth is, our worth has nothing to do with what we have and everything to do with who we are, and this is especially true for those who acquire wealth or power at the expense of others or who, through greed and the desire for more undermine the balance of nature. When the illusion of ownership takes priority; when we become obsessed with our possessions, life turns in on itself. Love and joy disappear, and all that's left is the ever-present struggle to exist.

Though we may not realize it, in a sense, the more we try to do the impossible and hold on to what we have, the smaller and more limited our lives become. Could it be when our time on earth ends, we will be remembered not so much for what we felt was ours but for what we did with what we had? In the realm of the eternal, a life well lived is measured not by how much we have but by how much we've given, how our lives have touched and made a difference in the lives of others. This is the greatest and only gift we can give to the world and the only thing we can take with us to our eternal home when our journey in this world comes to an end.

The Gift

Vital to the world of which we are a part is the life-sustaining properties of water. Through means natural and man-made, this gift, often taken for granted, provides the elements basic to all life.

Without it life as we know it could not exist. Like the air we breathe, water is everywhere. From gentle mists that creep silently up across the land on cool autumn mornings to spring showers that transform winter deserts into gardens of beauty. From rivers rushing towards the sea or oceans that divide continents to man-made lakes, canals, and city or county water systems, its magical powers create and support life in whatever form it appears.

As water sustains and refreshes the earth bringing fruit to bear and crops to harvest, so too does faith in giving direction and meaning to our lives. Through channels, both seen and unseen, the spirit of the Divine reaches out to the human, creating order out of chaos and harmony in place of discord.

New horizons and new possibilities appear. Landscapes once scarred and desolate through neglect or abuse are changed, and life again declares its presence. The mists of despair and loneliness begin to fade as the warmth and beauty of a new day begins.

Who Am I?

Down through the centuries, across cultures and continents, philosophers, theologians, and others from wisdom traditions have explored the meaning of existence. Though influenced and expressed through different languages and cultures, that search continues today. Without exception, each generation seeks to understand what's behind the mystery of this experience called life.

Upon entering the world, we had no idea what new adventure we were about to begin. We just knew we were here. There were others bigger and wiser who would take care of us and explain what life was all about.

In time as we moved from those formative years as children, we gradually became more self-conscious, more aware of who we were and our place in the world. Though seldom expressed directly, the question "who am I?" became a constant companion influencing our decisions and relationships.

As our journeys took us along new paths, some experiences were easy to accept, but others, though apparently needed, were not - the loss of a job, the separation or death of a companion or friend, struggles with an addiction, an unexpected accident or illness, financial challenges. No matter what the circumstances, each experience gave us the opportunity to reflect and to know ourselves and our relationships in ways we had not known before. Though subtle and seldom expressed, the question, "Who am I?" continued to weave itself in and out of every decision and experience.

In time many of us entered a new adventure called retirement. Once again, we had to redefine ourselves, for we were no longer identified by a particular career or profession, our worth or accomplishments. In a sense, this new experience was taking us back to a place and time where responsibilities were few, a place of dependence on others. For many, this was the most difficult transition, for it required us to explore deeper realities and truths that often conflicted with our traditions, culture, or religious backgrounds. The question of identity was once again very much a part of this new phase in our journey.

Reality was also reminding us of another truth not easy to accept. Time was no longer on our side as it was when we were younger. We were getting older. One by one, we said "goodbye" to friends and family, and we knew it would be our turn before long.

No matter who we were, how gifted or well off, soon we would have to leave behind everything we considered of value, not only our loved ones and our possessions but also those special interests and dreams we now knew we might never realize.

We were entering a period of transition where the known was beginning to fade, and the unknown was appearing in ways we could no longer avoid. We were at a crossroads between the here and now, our present reality and the eternal, experiencing the final moments of our journey. As time slipped by, fear of the unknown was gradually being replaced with an understanding of life in ways we had not understood before. "Who am I?" was even more persistent now.

Though it was not possible to avoid the inevitable, there was something deep within that was unwilling to accept the limitations of life as we knew it. We wondered. Could it be the journey we were now on was but one chapter in a life beyond the present? Could it be the limitations of existence in this world were but an illusion and the reality of life beyond the known was ours as well?

As our sense of the beyond became stronger, a power greater than ourselves made its presence known, speaking to our hearts of a life that had its beginnings in eternity and would continue throughout all the forevers yet to come. What we thought was an ending was not. We were about to enter a realm of existence unbounded by time that spanned the ages of eternity. The question "Who am I?" was about to take on new meaning … for a new adventure was about to begin.

Concepts For Living

Beyond life as we know it is a power that not only creates and supports life but is present in all that exists. It makes itself known in every heartbeat and every breath we take. It empowers us to be and do whatever we choose but will never override our personal desires or decisions.

Unlike the agendas our world has put in place, the purpose of the Creator is to provide a field where the spirit of love can be experienced and demonstrated. To live life as we were meant to, we must reach out and touch a reality beyond our own.

Performance and expectation are not part of the equation, for unconditional love has no requirements or expectations. It allows each freedom to think and act, to plan and become.

As we move to certain levels of awareness of our oneness with all that exists, we will cease our desires and efforts to get and control and will more freely allow life forces to flow through us in their ever-present journey towards renewal and change.

Though unseen, if our hearts and minds are open to the power that sustains all that exists, we will be brought to new heights in our journey that transcend the temporary and speak to us of some of life's deepest secrets and most profound truths.

New directions for living will take the place of past ventures which have led to pain and disappointment. Opportunities will be provided for becoming who we really are rather than what others think or expect. No longer will we need commendation and praise, nor fear criticism or condemnation. No longer will we be manipulated or controlled by anyone or anything outside ourselves.

Strength from within will give direction to our lives. Inner peace and validation rather than outward pressure or reward will become our experience. A new sense of freedom will be ours, the freedom to be who we were always meant to be – ourselves.

Let me surround you with all that I am, so you might realize all that you are.

A Force of Nature

Though often misunderstood and even more difficult to define, love plays a major role in what it means to be human. It's the source and power behind all that exists. Like some dynamic invisible force, this energy surrounds and is present throughout all creation. It knows no boundaries or anything that separates.

This creative power, the very nature of the Divine, affects all lives and all relationships. To completely understand or identify it may not be possible, but the importance of its presence cannot be denied. Without it, existence alone is all there is.

Early on, we begin to explore this powerful force. We are constantly being brought under its spell. Resistance is next to impossible. In a sense, we fall in love with love.

Unfortunately, this mysterious power can also be used to persuade or mislead for the sake of gain. Form and beauty are often emphasized at the expense of deeper issues and desires. From magazine covers to Hollywood movies, by word and through song, our imaginations are moved to buy certain products or expect romantic experiences out of touch with reality.

Though often used in ways that do more harm than good, this indescribable power affects every aspect of our lives. It surrounds and defines everything we are or ever shall be. It alone brings meaning to this adventure we are on.

Across the centuries, the greats of all time have tried to capture its essence, and though limited by its incomprehensible greatness, they have given us glimpses of its power and influence over the decisions we make, our relationships, and the directions our lives take.

Though some might question, it has been said that love is blind. Perhaps this is true or at least should be, especially at times in how we treat ourselves or allow others to treat us. Whether from childhood abuse or messages received that compromise our worth and integrity, most of us could not even begin to count the times we've gotten down on ourselves for our faults and failures or for not measuring up to what others expect.

Unfortunately, this way of thinking does little to help our self-worth or self-esteem. By continually looking at our imperfections or the expectations of others, we become our own worst enemy, fighting the very process meant to change us from who we think we are to the real person within.

Like a child learning to walk, we cannot expect to master the lessons life has to offer without trial and error or some resistance. Yes, there will be times when we fall and think we have failed, but falling is not failing. It is merely part of the process of learning to walk.

Life does not condemn us, nor does love, for falling. Instead, it encourages us – sometimes shouts at us – "Get up! Get up! You may have fallen, but you are not lost or forsaken. I am still here, and so are you. If you could see things as I do, you would understand all you have been through; everything that's happened from the day you entered the world until now is meant to lift you up, not tear you down."

Though we may not always sense His presence due to how intense our lives have become, we are not outcasts, nor are we abandoned. That would be impossible, for the Creator is never separate from that which He has created. During times of darkness or despair, pain or suffering, our minds may tell us otherwise, but that's an illusion, for we are never alone on this journey; we never have been and never will be.

Although we may not understand, the ability to not see, and be blind to what we consider our faults and failures, is not only in our self-interest but is also an attribute of the Divine. This incredible power, a love beyond comprehension, never judges or condemns that which He has created. He is fully aware of how we've been brought up, the circumstances under which we struggle, and the difficult experiences we've been through. He knows how helpless we feel at times, the fears that threaten us when we slip or fall or when the past comes up to haunt us with our mistakes and failures, but he also sees what we may not see … the power of love to transform.

Beyond what we are, He sees what we are becoming. He knows that our fears and struggles are just part of the process. They do not define us. Where we measure ourselves by how grownup we are or feel we should be, He sees an innocent little child loved beyond measure … a little person … just learning to walk.

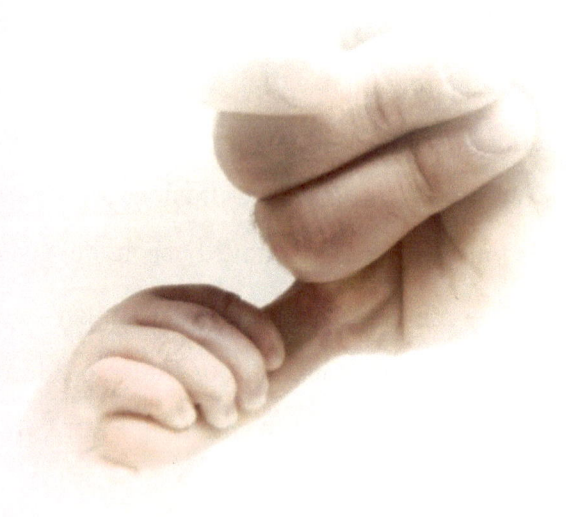

🕊 *It's easy to get lost when we forget where we came from.*

As The Years Go By

For many of us, the "golden years" leave a bit to be desired. The will to do, to dream may still be present, but the energy to do so may not. That which was done with ease in years past takes effort ... that is if it can be done at all.

As time slips by, what's really important takes on new meaning. Dreams not yet realized are left behind, and the reality of age with its limitations can no longer be ignored. Mother Nature ultimately has the final word, and neither wealth, power, nor prestige will silence her voice.

Not only does time slip by, but so do our memories. Our recall system may not work as efficiently as it used to. Names, places, and events that once could be recalled at a moment's notice are slow to come or disappear completely. Memories fade, and perhaps some should.

There's also a tendency to rely on the past as our identity, but no matter where we've been or what we've done, good or not so good, we are not the same today as we were. Life is like a kaleidoscope, ever-changing, and so are we. Like old clothes worn with pride, what once defined us now cannot.

Though challenges come with advanced years, new beginnings are also possible. Within each moment lies opportunities to begin again, to move in new directions, to choose new paths

Age may bring some limitations, but it's also a time of renewal, a time to learn, explore, to go on new adventures.

As the sun begins to sink below the horizon and the shadows gather, there's a sense that time is running out, and maybe that's so, but then again, maybe not. Could it be that where we sense an ending is but a new beginning, a transition into a new experience? Who knows, the finality of life we imagine just might not be as final as we think.

༒ *Outside of time, age does not exist.*

Beauty or the Beast

We live in a world obsessed with the external. To be strong and good-looking gives a person an edge on life, or so we are told. And since we all want to be successful, we try diets, exercise, new wardrobes, special beauty aids, and even surgery in order to be "forever young."

And the results? Mostly frustration. We still look like ourselves. There are the tall thin models and those a bit short and squashy. Some come with good-sized ears with feet and noses to match. There are the thick hairy types and the hair-free models. We are the sum-total of our parts, somewhat awkward and very human.

If only we could be transformed by some unique renovation process, recycled, or perhaps magically changed by a visit from our fairy godmother, then everything would be all right. If only beauty could be ours, how different life would be.

But beauty can be ours if we so choose. The only beasts that exist are those our imaginations have created. Regardless of height, weight, age, or gender, we are all beautiful.

Deep within the uniqueness of each of us lies rich resources of beauty. Love, joy, and compassion transcend the physical and give us a beauty of character that go far beyond any physical limitations we might have. It is this specialness coming from within that transforms the external and reminds us of how attractive we are and always have been.

No matter what we see in the mirror, how kind or unkind mother nature has been, our sense of beauty takes on new meaning when we look at ourselves and others from the heart. To share a quiet moment with a friend, laugh with a child, or embrace the one who is hurting with arms of love and a heart that understands, reflects a beauty of spirit that goes far beyond any external attractiveness or lack thereof.

Now You See Him – Now You Don't

To feel secure in a world that is anything but, is challenging enough for most of us. We manage; it's true if things go smoothly, but when life turns in on itself and everything that could go wrong ... does, we wonder. If there is a higher power, where is He when things get difficult when we need Him most?

No wonder, for many, a relationship with God seems so uncertain, so unreliable, and for some, so unreal. Is this how it was meant to be ... a game of hide and seek; now you see Him, now you don't? Could it be the One who is the parent to all parents has done something no loving earthly parents would ever do; give birth and then give up?

So where do we go from here? Who has the corner on truth? What if our parents, our children, or our friends choose a path different than ours? Are they wrong? Who wins? Who loses? Who has the final word?

Though some might think otherwise, all of us are conditioned to live within the bounds of the cultural values and religious or non-religious beliefs in which we are born. We are all products of the time and circumstances under which we enter the universe. There are no exceptions.

So, what do we do; which way do we turn when voices everywhere try to convince us their way, their truth is the one and only way of communicating with God and the only right path to the hereafter? Who has the answers?

It has been said that if the most commonly accepted concepts and theological insights from all religions, philosophers, and wisdom traditions, both ancient and modern, were put together in an attempt to understand God, they would fall infinitely short of even beginning to comprehend that power that has brought all that is into existence. And though this may be true, and our ability to understand is limited, down through the ages, the Creator has continually tried to reveal Himself in ways consistent with what we are familiar and ready to receive.

Sacred scriptures and other inspired sources have suggested that the creator is constantly communicating with all to whom He has given life, that it's not a matter of with whom He communicates but who is listening. Could this be a truth worth looking into?

Though often ridiculed, marginalized, or worse, there have been those throughout history from different backgrounds and traditions who have found a way of reconnecting to their higher power; ordinary people who have done extraordinary things. Through their own experience, they have been instrumental in transforming the lives of others. Some have even changed the course of nations.

Are we less worthy than they? Is the creator selective ... some meant to hear his voice, and others not? Perhaps it's time we reassessed our part in the communication process. Is it possible we are so conditioned to listening to the voices of authority figures or giving priority to our "to-do" list that the still small voice within is silenced or ignored?

Back before memory, we felt secure for nine months in our connection to the source of life until we entered the world; then, suddenly, everything changed. The security and oneness we once knew were no longer there. We were in a strange new world, alone and helpless. Though symbolic, could it be this sense of separation at birth has continued in one form or another in our relationship with God, to ourselves, and to those with whom we share this journey?

To not only restore but give meaning to relationships is what life is all about. It's a gradual process. We cannot know what it's like to be warm if we've never been cold. Light cannot be appreciated or understood without darkness, nor can joy without sorry, or pleasure without pain. How can we know what it's like to be found if we've never been lost, succeed if we haven't known failure? What is a mountaintop experience without valleys of depression or despair?

All relationships and experiences we go through provide us opportunities to become who we were always meant to be rather than what our societies, our families, or others have told us about ourselves. This is especially true for those who have chosen to share their journey with another.

Does this mean a close relationship is always easy? Some say it is, or at least that's the way it should be, but reality often suggests otherwise.

Even in the closest, most committed relationships, there will be times when we might get irritated or even angry at the person we love the most and share life with. Who do they think they are confronting us with our irrational behavior or inconsistent way of doing things?

Though it may be to our benefit, it is never easy or comfortable to see ourselves as we really are in the eyes of a friend or companion rather than who we think we are.

Of course, all relationships, especially those that become lifelong and are the most helpful, begin somewhere, normally as a friendship. Important though it may be to develop a deep and lasting friendship with someone with whom we share our journey, it is not an overnight experience. It takes commitment and time for any relationship to become more than a wave or a handshake.

Could it be a friendship with God is similar, that it takes a certain level of commitment? If, as it has been said, the Eternal continues to communicate as He did in days of old, what is it that stands in our way of hearing His voice? Is it possible our lives have become so intense, so distracted by the superficial, that the time required for restoring this connection is just not available?

Though some of us have more and others less of the resources we consider important in life, we all share one resource in common – time! Because it's limited however, its' worth is far greater than we realize. What we do with it and how we use it is up to us. For those who invest wisely, the dividends can be substantial. For others who do not see its value, considerably less, if anything at all.

As in any human relationship, communication with the creator also takes time. We cannot know Him nor truly know ourselves without allowing the time needed for that relationship to develop. Without doubt, life has become more intense now than in the past. To squeeze anything additional into busy schedules beyond what is required is difficult but not impossible. Actually, we do it all the time. If we feel it's important enough, we somehow "find the time." Is it not possible to do the same in reconnecting with the one who has given us life?

Few of us will have the opportunity, nor would we want to go beyond our personal or professional lives to live in a more secluded environment in order to strengthen our spiritual experience, but we can all find some time to renew what should be our primary relationship.

Connection with the beyond is still possible. A relationship with God and the ways to do so have no limits. The only limits are in our minds.

Everything and everyone around us provide these opportunities. For instance, at birth, each of us was given membership in one of the greatest, grandest cathedrals of all – the world of nature. We are surrounded by the beauty and mystery of a world that can take our breath away. Nothing compares.

Time alone for a few moments or a few hours sitting by a lake or in a field surrounded by wildflowers at the beginning or end of the day can make a difference. Listening to a song or walking along a beach with the wind touching our faces and the sound of waves crashing at our feet can awaken the spirit within. Holding a hand, reading a book, watching a beautiful sunrise or breathing in the fragrance of a flower; playing with a child, or hearing the innocent cry of a newborn can bring new life to the soul. Even a few minutes taken to call a loved one or have coffee with a friend can make a difference. If we are conscious and awake to the voice of the natural world around us, all of nature will whisper truths to our hearts that can uplift and reconnect us to each other and to our Creator.

With the exception of relationships formed for convenience or other reasons, love is the primary energy that brings people together. Though the romantic aspect of love is exciting and should never be discounted, it alone is not enough. Very soon after a relationship is formed, couples begin to realize these beautiful, handsome forms they have been attracted to have real people inside, and these people don't always agree with one another.

Gradually things begin to change. Not everything is the same as it was at the beginning. There is a different feel to the relationship, sometimes close, sometimes not. There's a transition to new ways of thinking and new ways of doing things - a household to manage, a family to provide for, responsibilities at work, children to take care of, emergency situations to deal with, financial needs, and around almost every corner - the unexpected. Add to this getting to know each other better under circumstances or in situations that are not always ideal, and the challenges are far from ordinary. How these differences and challenges are met will eventually determine the future of the relationship ... if there is one.

Although we would like it to be different, is it possible a relationship with God is similar, sometimes close ... sometime not? Could it be what appears to us a game of "hide and seek," "now you see him, now you don't," is but a misunderstanding of what a relationship with God should look like?

To think that any relationship will remain constant all the time is unreal. Such experiences do not exist, even in the lives of those who are the most centered, the most spiritual.

Life is like a grand composition. It has rhythm, highs, and lows, good times and not so good, times when we feel close and other times not, like a dance ... together – apart, together – apart.

Mountain-top experiences will come, but so will the valleys. Though we wonder, could it be, like the changing seasons, everything we go through is meant for our good, that life and love have many dimensions we are meant to feel and express, experience, and explore?

To believe we have lost our way, that God has abandoned us because life does not present itself in the way we want or expect, is far from the truth. There are no perfect paths or perfect people. We are all on a journey exploring the unknown. Regardless of how stormy or difficult the way, relationships built on love, human or divine, will survive.

Though they lived under different circumstances and at different times, some of the greatest minds and most revered spiritual leaders, past and present, have described God as not only the source of love but the one who loves unconditionally, a concept which for most of us is not only difficult to understand but almost impossible to accept.

It would seem by what we've been taught and the way we live that God's love and acceptance are anything but unconditional. After all, isn't everything around us based on meeting certain conditions? Wouldn't God expect the same?

We have learned, have we not? When the going gets rough, like some magical entity, God may appear with temporary relief but then disappears. It's an on-again, off-again relationship, and we just have to get used to it. If we want to make God happy and have a better relationship with him, then certain expectations and conditions are required; otherwise, there can be no rewards in this world or the world to come.

Is this how it was meant to be, or is it possible God's love is just as unconditional today as it has always been, that the only requirements are those we have been conditioned to believe? Could it be that we are accepted just the way we are, that unconditional love is ... well ... actually ... unconditional?

Though often ridiculed, discredited, or worse, as far back as memory allows, voices from the past from different cultures and traditions have spoken about a love both divine and eternal that never condemns, has no limits, and is completely unconditional, a love which allows each life form the freedom to express itself and become whatever it chooses.

Even though, at times, we may feel alone or abandoned, that can never be. He who brings life into being surrounds us with his presence with a love that is forever and unconditional. That the Creator would intentionally put in place a system of communication with His children that creates instability and fear is totally opposed to the principles of love upon which the universe is based. Every breath we take and every heartbeat is a statement of God's presence and His desire to have a personal relationship with each of his children. The only requirement is a heart that is open and a mind willing to respond.

We are all children learning to walk. We may slip, fall, say or do things we regret, and act in ways that hurt ourselves, others, or those we love the most. At times we've chosen the convenient over what's best and made decisions that have put ourselves or others in difficult situations.

None of us are entirely proud of our actions, past or present, nor exempt from the temptations and challenges we share in common. We know what it's like to wrestle with thoughts and feelings that are on the dark side and with addictions or certain patterns of behavior that contradict the person we long to be and really are.

Times will come when we feel deserted and alone, guilty or unworthy, with little hope beyond the continual struggle to exist, but we are not alone and never have been. This is a journey shared. We are not orphans, forsaken, or forgotten. The great Creator of all, who is the beginning and end of all that exists, is always present with us surrounding us with a love that has no conditions, never judges, and never condemns; a love that has the power to transform and carry us through to a future beyond anything we could ever imagine.

The "Present"

Acceptance of the past and hope for a better tomorrow is not something we should dismiss or ignore; however, in reality, neither the past nor the future really exists except in our minds. The past is gone forever, and the future is yet to be. We can learn from the past and look forward to the future, but we can't live there. A life lived in the present is the only reality we have.

Only the present provides opportunities to begin a new adventure, explore the unknown, or try something dreamed about but never realized. Regardless of the past, good times, or regrets, the possibilities in the present are unlimited, not only to try something new but to begin again.

In a sense, the present is just that, a "present," a gift – 24 hours to use any way we wish. Each day, each moment, if invested wisely, is like a precious stone whose beauty and worth only increase as time goes by.

To embrace life in the here and now, no matter how it presents itself, can transform the ordinary into the extraordinary and can make each moment that follows a window of opportunity into all the "today's" that follow.

> ❦ There is no
>   greater gift
>   than the "present."

Who Says I Have to Be Right

How important is it to be "right?" Is it okay to be "wrong?" Is it a sign of weakness to admit we don't always have the right answers? Does being wrong make us less than who we should be? Do we feel intimidated or imperfect if we don't always say or do the right thing?

Being human involves a recognition and acceptance of our strengths and limitations, that we don't know it all and never will. It also means being aware of how much each of us is influenced by our backgrounds, our understanding of life, and the experiences we go through. To be human means what's "right" for me may be totally "wrong" for you.

An emphasis on being right that overrides the human spirit is destructive. It alienates friends, sacrifices relationships, and destroys families. When emphasized beyond its importance, it can drain the very heart out of life and make us more like pawns than people. Although appearances may indicate otherwise, if examined closely, it might at times be more akin to pride and fear or a desire to be "perfect."

To reach out in love and kindness to those in need. To give a helping hand to someone less fortunate than ourselves. To be open and honest with ourselves and others brings a new dimension to our lives and our relationships that will outdistance any of our "rightness" or righteousness.

Learning to be who we are, and allowing others to be themselves, is what really matters, regardless of who's "right" or who's "wrong."

Though gradual and subtle, our understanding of right and wrong changes over time.

A Celebration in Time

To celebrate life is as natural as the air we breathe, the next heartbeat, or the beauty of a sunrise. All of nature responds to the awesomeness of the world in which we live.

Life may not always appear as we would like, but it is magnificent. Every flower, every blade of grass, and every sunset are statements of the beauty that surrounds us. It can be seen in the majesty of an eagle in flight or the gentle coo of a dove. It speaks to our hearts at the dawn of a new day, the laughter of a child or a rainbow after a storm, in snowflakes swirling around our feet, in the rain that dances on our face, or even in the more difficult, challenging experiences we go through.

It's the all of everything, both seen and unseen, in an infinite universe of universes, a song from the eternal sung and celebrated since the dawn of creation.

All of life, from its humblest form to its grandest, was meant to be part of this song of the ages. There are no requirements, only invitations. Individual choice is always honored, never demanded or compromised.

Only when the mists of illusion begin to clear, and a higher level of consciousness takes its place, can deeper realities be understood and new possibilities realized. When we change, when we see and feel our connection to everyone and everything around us, then the universe changes as well, pulling us out of ourselves back into harmony with the rhythm of life. We will then intuitively understand that everything, no matter how difficult, whether mountaintop experiences or valleys of despair, are meant for our good.

As our hearts open to accept the gifts life has to offer, we will understand that everything we go through is meant to be. Each experience, from birth to our final goodbye, has its purpose. Each has a place in the story of our lives. All are part of the grand mosaic of experiences that make us who we are.

When we take time to back away from the routine and reconnect to that power that brought all that is into existence, the dawn of a new day will begin, and we will appear as we were always meant to be – beings of eternal value transformed and transforming those around us. The wonder of it all and the possibilities of whom we might become will bring us a sense of joy at times so overwhelming that we will know no other response but that of celebration.

As a lake reflects the beauty of that which surrounds it, so too will our lives reflect that by which we choose to be surrounded.

Everyday Heroes

We call them heroes when ordinary people do extraordinary things in emergency situations, but they don't see themselves as extraordinary. Most respond with, "I just did what was needed like anyone else would have done."

Like these down-to-earth "heroes," few of us would forsake a friend or even a stranger when the going gets rough, but unfortunately, we often neglect and even get "down on" one of the most amazing people anywhere – ourselves.

To be there for others when needed is a wonderful statement about the human spirit, however, we must first move beyond feelings of guilt and shame our minds and others have placed upon us; otherwise our response to the needs of others will be limited.

Whether in emergency situations or not, love and respect for ourselves must come first if we expect to have an influence for good on those around us. Words can help and heal, but far and beyond words is a greater gift we can provide others – the gift of ourselves.

Perhaps it's time we were reminded again about someone very special – you! You may have forgotten, but there is only one "you" in the entire universe. You are one-of-a-kind, an original. You may not be all you'd like to be, but you're getting there. Be yourself. Embrace the uniqueness of who you are and who you're becoming. Be a gift, a present to yourself. Then and only then can you truly be a gift to others.

*🕊 Unity comes about through
cooperation,
not competition.*

Being A Part of the Team

No matter the rules or who's on the team, we are all involved in the game of life. Whether we win or lose is not the concern but how we play and how we relate to others on the team, especially when they don't always see "eye-to-eye" with us.

Can we support them and encourage them? And what if they fail to measure up to our "game plan?" Is it okay for them to have opinions or ideas different than ours? Are their thoughts still of value?

Whether we look at the automotive industry, a supermarket chain, or a small family-owned business, good equipment is only useful when the components that make up the technology are integrated, working together as they were designed.

So it is, even with ordinary folks like you and me. When we work together, our strengths and abilities, even our weaknesses seen in a different light are very powerful and can accomplish far more than we might realize. One person alone can do very little, but together we're always successful. We always "win," ... even if we don't always agree.

> *Criticism pulls people down,
> but they fly on the wings of praise.*

To Be or Not to Be

What's a person worth? Is it measured by how much they know, whom they know, or how successful they are? Where does advanced education or certain titles fit in? Does fame, fortune, or good looks give an advantage? What does it take to make us feel satisfied with ourselves, comfortable with who we are?

Could it be that our real value has more to do with who we are than what we accomplish, how wealthy, or how well educated? Is it possible what we think of ourselves is more important than what others think?

To love and appreciate ourselves is not selfishness. It's a celebration of our humanness, our uniqueness, and the place each of us has in this grand, amazing universe.

All of us are special and worthy of life's greatest gifts. To look at ourselves as being anything less undermines the tremendous potential we've been given as human beings.

As we learn to love and accept ourselves just the way we are, we will be empowered to reach out to others giving them the courage to accept and love themselves just the way they are.

"To be or not to be?" is not just a question. It's a way of life.

🕊 *The only way to open the heart is to still the mind.*

The Me That I Am

Life is an amazing adventure with some great opportunities. Unfortunately, many of us get so caught up in family expectations or certain messages from our society that we end up contributing far less to life than we could. Feelings of inadequacy or inferiority instilled in childhood or later in life overshadow our gifts and abilities and make us smaller than who we really are.

Rather than coming from a place of self-confidence, we often turn to an "if only" approach. If only I had been born under different circumstances, had a different family or better environment. If only opportunities had come my way, like my brother or that person over there.

If only …

And so it goes, but it doesn't get us very far. No matter how sincere our desires, life rarely falls into line with our wishes or our demands. We don't shape life. Life shapes us. Fair or not, life comes to us as it comes. Our place is to make decisions, respond to whatever we face, and make the best of conditions or situations we meet, desirable or not.

Very few, if any of us came into this world under ideal circumstances. To some extent, we're all limited. All of us face situations that are difficult to deal with. At times we are amazed at how far we've come, all we've done, and how successful we've been, but there are times too, when we don't do as well as we'd like. We falter, we fail, we fall. We end up on detours, heading in directions and experiencing things we never expected or desired.

Perhaps it would be good for us to take a closer look at this adventure we're on. Maybe it's time we moved past the illusions that imprison us and embrace a new reality. The truth is we don't need to be limited by what others say or think. No matter what comes our way, each new day provides opportunities for us to make new decisions that allow us to know and become who we were always meant to be. We may have a way to go, and that will always be true, but we're making progress, and that's enough, at least for today.

And The Truth Shall Make You Free

The desire to be free, free to explore and celebrate life in whatever form it presents itself, is primary if life is to be experienced as it was meant to be.

Regardless of our backgrounds, freedom is the birthright of us all. It has no ties to a particular religion, tradition or philosophy, nor does it have any political boundaries. It goes beyond the restrictions imposed by national pride or personal preference. It releases us from the past, frees us to live in the present, and prepares us for a future of unlimited possibilities.

True freedom is a gift to be experienced and celebrated. It is much more than the rights or privileges provided by allegiance to a particular country or race. It's an experience from within, a deeper reality unaffected by outside influences.

Unfortunately, the right to be free, to express ourselves openly is often limited by cultural directives or by authority figures whose influences overshadow or weaken personal beliefs and desires. No matter what the source, when outside influences undermine the abilities and talents we've inherited, causing us to be less than who we are, the benefits to others and ourselves also become limited.

As a flower shares its beauty and fragrance with all who pass by, so too are we meant to make a difference in the lives of those around us. We, too, are endowed with gifts and talents meant to enrich the lives of others. By simply being ourselves, we encourage others to be who they really are. In a sense, we set them free, free to be themselves, free to be the gifted creative beings they were meant to be, free to express themselves in whatever way they wish.

Throughout the natural world, there are no restrictions. Nature has no boundaries, for control does not exist. Life lived in whatever form it appears is ever-changing and evolving. Regardless of winter storms and times of drought, the earth continues to endure and evolve. Branches bent and bare, beaten by the elements, come back to life again every spring. Early morning mists and gentle rains refresh the earth, and once again, new life appears. Flowers bloom while birds of every description wing their way across the heavens, flying where they will, building their nests wherever they choose. No matter where life exists or in what form, each species is free to roam, to go where their instincts take them, build their dens or nests wherever they want, free to express themselves in whatever way they wish.

As explorers, we share this adventure called life with our fellow travelers, and we will not fail, but our progress can be slowed by the voices in our minds that drag us down, enslave us through fear or addiction, and tell us who we are not. It is only as we reconnect to the deeper places within, allowing our minds to be servants to our souls; then and only then can healing take place and the freedom of spirit we so much desire and deserve be experienced.

Darkness May Come,
But So Does the Dawn

The difficult experiences in life we all face eventually come to an end, and though we sometimes wonder, we will survive them.

No one can truly appreciate sunshine without rain, joy without sorrow, or pleasure without pain. Life's "ups and downs," hard times and happy times, loves and losses give balance to our lives and help us grow.

Troubles like tears are meant to cleanse. They help us see better. They push and pull us. They make us reflect. They reshape us. If allowed, they add insight and wisdom to our lives.

No matter how long the night, dawn always comes. Its beauty and brightness transform the landscapes of our lives, and in time we will know that all is well.

We can learn from the past, but when the past is allowed to control, it compromises the present and casts a shadow over the future.

The Road to Success

Our entry into the world may not have been recognized as those born into fame or fortune, but no matter how ordinary or humble our beginnings, the possibilities of a life well lived may reach far beyond the circumstances of our birth. Who knows what's packaged inside a new addition to the world or what that little person might accomplish in years to come.

Regardless of class, privilege, or the generosity of heredity, every life has potential. All are born with gifts and abilities once developed that can make a difference in the lives of others.

No matter how limited, all of us want to accomplish something that gives meaning and direction to our lives. The challenge is how to get from where we are to where we'd like to be. Is there a way of measuring how well we've done, some magic formula? Does status or financial advantage guarantee success for some and limit others?

How does the universe recognize who has "made it" and who has not? Which life form is worthy of recognition, honored above the rest? Is it the bird that soars the highest or the dog that barks the loudest? Who comes out on top, the horse that runs the fastest or the duck that swims the farthest? Who is recognized as contributing the most, the street sweeper faithfully doing her job or the CEO managing a company of a thousand people? Who decides? Who gives the final word on how far we've come, how much we've accomplished?

Perhaps we need to re-access the standards used to measure worth. Maybe there are other ways to evaluate a person's contribution to life beyond what we've been told by our traditions or our societies. Is it possible what we now see as a grand achievement may, in time, look different, and where we've struggled, lost the battle, and ended up going in a direction totally unexpected is actually just what was needed to move us to the next level in our journey?

As the purpose of life becomes clearer and we more fully understand our relationship to all creation, that which is of real value will change. We will know inherently that what really matters is not the accumulation of matter but living a life that matters. No longer will we be possessed by our possessions, our success determined by position or profession, or how well we perform, but by how our lives have made a difference in the world around us and the lives of those who have shared our journey. Such a life well lived can never fail to succeed.

Success is defined by how much we love, not how much we know.

Common Ground

Life is an amazing adventure, but there are times when it gets in the way of what we expect or what we've been taught. Just when we're feeling satisfied with who we are and where we are, the unexpected appears out of nowhere and throws us off balance.

Even though we might be pleased with our lives the way they are, the great Creator might not see things the way we do. His purpose for bringing us into existence was never meant to encourage or support a life with little or no responsibility. Life was designed as an ever-evolving experience, an on-going relationship to all that exists, including and especially to our fellow travelers.

Like a mirror the unseen, of which the seen is merely a reflection, has little concern about our comfort or what's convenient. Yes, along the way there will be special experiences to celebrate with family and friends and times of renewal that nature provides, but a life of ease ... sleepwalking through life ... is not part of the plan.

Life is anything but constant. It comes at us from every direction. No one is exempt. It disturbs. It disrupts. It cares little about how hard we've worked or the plans we have so carefully put in place. Without warning storms come from nowhere. Things begin to fall apart. We feel disoriented or worse. Before we know it, we're moving in a direction totally opposite our plans with no idea where we're going.

Crossroads ... times of crisis come to all. The desire to reach out to find some security during times of unrest in a world that offers little is understandable but often the support chosen is unreliable. Thoughts expressed such as "we're all in this together," accepted by many, doesn't always ring true. We're conditioned to believe, however, that if the words are repeated loud enough and long enough, in some mystical, magical way, everything will turn out all right. Unfortunately, no matter how sincere, how pleasant the words or how well received, they are often out of touch with reality.

Situations come when we feel overwhelmed ... alone ... not sure which way to turn. "No one understands what I'm going through," expresses how we really feel, especially true for those of us who entered life under circumstances far from ideal, who had little voice as to the families we were born into and who now live out the results.

Many of us know all too well what it's like to be brought up in environments where discipline and abuse were primary and love all but absent. Those early years which should have provided encouragement to young minds and bodies were either rare or absent altogether. Alcohol or drugs may or may not have played a part, but the results of certain family structures, religious or non, where decisions were dictated rather than encouraged, obedience required without reason or love having a voice, did little to prepare young lives for future responsibilities.

Because a strong foundation in early childhood was anything but desirable and blind obedience was all they knew, many of the young reach adulthood acting in ways that are anything but mature. They live out what they've been taught as do their children and without change, future generations will follow. They are little people in adult bodies and the decisions they make at home and in their professional lives are a reflection of what they have learned.

Many of our leaders today who have been put in positions of trust, in business or elected to offices of service have allowed greed, power and control to dominate their lives ... and the decisions they make reflect their immaturity. They mistake power for strength and control for freedom. They are but children disguised as adults.

Though the exception, whether in leadership positions or not, there are those brought up in families with limited or no support, who have learned from those early years. They don't want to relive those experiences again nor do they want their children to. They are the ones with the courage to break the cycle, who have chosen a new way and help others do the same.

Even though most of us come from reasonably stable backgrounds, none of us are exempt from certain influences that need to be addressed for we are each part of the human experience, continually dealing with situations meant to bring us to new levels of understanding. Our journeys take us to places of beauty, and experiences that lift the spirit, but there will also be rivers to cross, mountains to climb and barren terrain to get through.

Though we might wish otherwise, no one can reach higher levels of consciousness without going through times of disappointment, struggle and pain. These are the elements that refine and reform. Without them we may exist, but progress will be limited.

Whether from a religious perspective or from some other source, we are continually reaching out to whoever or whatever to find some sense of stability. Unfortunately, we may never find it, at least not in the way we would like. Though unaware, everything around us is gradually changing, becoming, evolving into something else and we are part of that process. Who we are now is not who we will be tomorrow or even in the next ten minutes.

No matter what the circumstances when we entered the world or how difficult just to accept "what is" or the extreme opposite ... fight to get what we want ... will not get us very far. We have been told life is a "battle and a march" and at times that's the way it seems, or at least that's what our minds tell us, but to allow our minds or the thoughts of others to have the final word on how we approach or experience life may not be in our best interest.

Yes, we might want to think things through, "use our heads" but when the mind is given priority over the heart and spirit ... that which is in our best interest, what we really desire and need ... may not be realized. Without intuition and insight, the mind is not enough and was never meant to be the final word on how we live or the direction our lives take. When the mind alone is in control, the outcome is obvious. All we have to do is look at history or the world we have created today to see the results.

Though by no means easy, the process of renewal, of becoming more conscious, is not a matter of surrender as we understand it ... like those defeated in battle, their rights or even their lives taken away, but rather surrender to a power greater than ourselves who restores not destroys.

This process is a daily experience, not meant to honor the ego in order to get what we want, but a willingness to give the Creator priority in guiding the decisions we make regardless of how small, so we might receive and experience not what we want but what we need and more. As this process proceeds, in time we will come to understand that what we need is really what we wanted all the time but just didn't realize.

In a sense, though not conscious of what we are doing, on some level all of us are into power and control. We may not remember, but we began life that way. If our needs were not met right away, there were tears, anger, a tantrum or two … and in time, when our feelings were translated into words, we made it clear … "that toy is mine, not yours. Give it back … or …" As we got older, nothing much changed. Our toys just get bigger and so did our rights, our demands and our desires to protect it all.

To give up power and control is not easy for there is much we've been taught and much we have to unlearn. We've been conditioned from childhood on to believe our ability to survive, to succeed is up to us. We are the masters of our destiny and though there is some truth to this idea, it cannot stand alone.

As already mentioned, for most of us the word "surrender" means defeat, rights taken away, subjugation to another, some form of slavery … or worse. Though we are slow to learn, it's meaning is entirely different when it comes to a relationship between the human and the divine.

God has no desire to take anything away from us that's not in our best interest, only that which stands in our way of becoming the person we want to be and who we were always meant to be. Surrender to a Power greater than ourselves is not a defeat but a victory. It's letting go of the "I" being the primary voice in the decisions we make, the directions our lives take and allowing the One who knows what is best under all circumstances, to have the final word.

No, this shift, victory through surrender, will not be an overnight experience. As with the physical, so it is with the spiritual, restoration takes time. There is much to learn and much we've learned we must leave go of. Because of backgrounds that have undermined the human spirit, this process will be more difficult for some than for others. There are many who every day fight with depression, certain patterns of behavior or the injuries they received in early years who try to escape through drugs, alcohol or addictions that undermine their relationships and for some, even their very existence.

Though we may be unaware, the Creator of the created is never absent from his children nor is he ever caught off guard by their failures or behavior. He has a long history of working with the discouraged, the lost and forgotten, those marginalized by society who have all but given up.

In a sense "we're all in this together" is true for this adventure we're on is a shared experience. Our stories, our relationships, our professions may be different. We may have lived or our journeys taken us to places that have shaped our lives through traditions or by cultures in ways unexpected but we are all members of the same family. We are human "beings" … ever changing … becoming … always in transition.

We stand on common ground. Regardless of status, advantage or disadvantage, no one is ever forgotten; no one is ever left behind. We are all part of the process of moving from darkness to light, from the unknown to the known, to new levels of understanding, of a consciousness that sees the Divine in ourselves, in others and everything around us.

We may not be all we would like to be, but we are becoming ... changing and as we allow a Power greater than ourselves to have a voice in the decisions we make and the directions our lives take, the results will be far greater than anything we might attempt to do on our own.

Progress not perfection is what the journey is all about. Like those of the past and those who will follow ... we are weak ... we are strong ... we are human! We may never completely overcome certain patterns of behavior, addictive thoughts or actions, but we cannot fail for we are surrounded by a love that is eternal, a love that transforms ... a love that says ... I am enough ... and so are you!

Face to Face

It has been said "actions speak louder than words," and it's true, often in ways far greater than we realize.

We may say little or nothing, but our eyes don't lie, nor is it easy to hide our feelings. A smile, a tear, a frown; all are expressions of thoughts or feelings we embrace or concerns we have.

To try and hide from each other doesn't work very well. Our faces are the playground of every emotion, a reflection of whatever we're thinking or going through. They reveal more about ourselves than we realize.

If we are willing to move beyond the imaginary walls that separate us, beyond the electronic and impersonal, and actually be there for one another, a new way of thinking and living begins to take shape. Feelings of separation begin to fade. It finally dawns on us. We have never been alone and never will be. Life is a journey shared.

Coming face to face with ourselves and others transform each experience, especially so when we recognize the creative power behind all that exists. Unless and until we look beyond the seen, into the face of the unseen, and understand our connection to all life in whatever form it appears, we will continue to live the illusion of separation as real and the reality of our oneness as an illusion.

Regardless of our backgrounds, where we were born, how well off we are, or what we look like, we are all members of the human family with responsibilities and privileges shared by all. We're on a journey together into the unknown, and it's this "togetherness," this sense of oneness, that will see us through no matter what life brings our way.

> *When you look at My face, you will see your own. When you seek my power, you will discover your own.*

Life is For-giving, Not For-getting

Across the centuries, as far back as written records allow, history has remembered those few who stood out from the rest, not only those in positions of prestige and power but those too of simple means and humble backgrounds whose insight and creative spirit were far in advance of their time.

Seldom did their lives conform to the ways generally accepted by the majority, for they were on a different path. They were unwilling to follow the cultural directives and mandates of their society, for theirs was a reality that went far beyond the thinking of the times in which they lived. They understood the insights given them were not their own but that of a power greater than themselves.

They lived life differently than the majority, misunderstood by most of the great minds of their time. Their approach to life often became the subject of laughter or contempt. Many were looked at as misfits, outcasts of society, and ridiculed or worse. Some were imprisoned; others gave their lives for their beliefs; some were even crucified, yet today they are honored as pioneers, visionaries, saviors whose insight has helped thousands avoid disaster and opened up new possibilities for the human race.

These pioneers of old were not perfect, nor were their messages, but the connection they had to a power greater than themselves and their willingness to follow a path not chosen by most has changed the lives of thousands, and a few have even altered the course of nations.

At a very deep level, they understood that life was not for getting but for giving. Though most were not aware at the time, their lives were a gift not only to their generation but to generations to come.

Our lives, too, can become a blessing, a gift to those around us, for we can never lose that which we give away. If, however, we embrace the bigger, better, more message of our society, if our lives become centered on getting rather than giving, obsessed with possessing rather than blessed by providing, our lives will become smaller, and the good we could have done will never be realized. Life will then become a battle and a march, turning in on itself. Love and joy will disappear, and what will remain is the ever-present struggle to exist.

To use our gifts, financial or otherwise, to benefit those whose needs are greater than our own, to help them reach their dreams when we can see the results, is far better than coming to the end of the journey and being forced to give up everything.

Though names may fade from memory, the results of a life dedicated to those in need will never be forgotten.

So choose wisely. Make of your life a gift. Stoop low; lift up the fallen, and you too will be lifted up. Bind up the wounds of the injured, and you too will be healed. Comfort those who sorrow and you too will be comforted. Help those who are distressed or addicted to overcome, and you too will overcome.

When the needs of others are honored, your needs too will be met. Life will then become a grand adventure, a celebration in time, an experience far greater than anything you could ever imagine.

Life is measured not so much on the expanse of time as it is on the eternity of the moment.

If Only

How easy it is to blame others for our unhappiness or our failures. If only she had responded as she should have, everything would be fine. If only I had been brought up in a better family. If only my companion, my children, my friends had been there for me as they could have been, then ...

Most of us have quite a few "if only's" to lean on, but they don't get us very far. No matter how difficult the past, the present can be different if we so choose. Taking responsibility for the decisions we make may take courage, but it will get us much further than the "if only" approach.

To be honest, the truth is no one really stands in our way except ourselves. It might be well for us to remember again the words passed down by the original inhabitants of this great land of ours. "We have met the enemy, and he is us!"

🦋 *Expect nothing; embrace everything.*

Treasures in Time

No matter how strong our faith may be in the world to come, the only reality we know is where we are now. Life on earth is one of movement, transition, and change. How quickly time goes by. Hours turn to days and days to years in the blink of an eye. From childhood and adolescence to old age, time moves on at a pace that almost takes our breath away.

If only we could turn the clock back a bit or at least slow it down, but we don't have that option. Time marches on regardless of our wishes or demands.

But we can slow down if we wish. Time can be a servant instead of a master if we so choose. Here and there, scattered throughout our lives, are special moments, treasures in time that are ours for the taking. All we have to do is be open to their presence; accept and embrace them as they come to us through the unexpected and the ordinary.

There's the innocent smile of a child. The fresh scent of new life after a storm. An unexpected call or card from a friend. The intimate caress of a gentle breeze on a warm summer's night. A thought, a smile, a touch from someone who cares, or a walk through silvery shadows on a cloudless star-filled night.

To all who choose to live life fully, time is a friend, not an enemy. Time spent in an intimate relationship with life renews life.

No matter how hard we try, we can't make time stand still, but in the stillness of the moment, we can find riches of far more value than any of our professional accomplishments or anything we might possess.

And so, our journeys continue, moving us ever closer to our destination. To be aware of where we've been and where we're going is important, but even more important is our understanding of the journey itself. To experience and celebrate our adventures along the way is what makes life worth living and the destination worth reaching.

At times we miss seeing the beauty around us because we're looking in the wrong direction.

Life is an infinitely short journey between two eternities. What we make of it is what matters.

So How Do We Measure Up?

Besides what is passed on to us through heredity, every aspect of our lives is influenced by the social and religious environments in which we live. Gradually our lives are shaped and our identities defined by the messengers and messages we receive.

We've been told our success or failure in life is largely determined by how much we have and our potential for acquiring more. This system of measurement has been ingrained into our thinking and influences every aspect of our lives. It tells us what we must do, what we should buy, and how to express ourselves. It has allowed what we have in our pockets to determine our self-worth and our place in society.

This manmade system of measurement has been given such power that it has become the standard by which our whole world operates. Beyond the purchasing power it allows, it has even been used in some situations to determine matters of life and death and is seen by many as the arbiter of destiny. It provides tremendous opportunity for some and little for others.

But what if this method of measurement didn't exist; how then would we live? By what means or standards would we evaluate a person's worth? How would we know the value of anything? And what about opportunities? Who would be among the favored, and who not?

Could it be there are advanced civilizations in other parts of the universe that provide adequately for their inhabitants without using self-made systems of measurement?

The possibilities are good; however such a transition for our world would take insight and effort and would involve a process that breaks through the illusion of separation and competition.

To adopt a new system meant to replace our existing methods of investment and trade would require a new way of thinking, one that honors each member of the human family; that recognizes and respects all.

This new approach - buying, selling, giving, and receiving - would not be an overnight experience and would require thought processes foreign to most and resisted by many.

If it were to succeed, an understanding of life as a shared experience must become the prism through which earth's resources are managed, no longer claimed by the few at the expense of the many, but distributed equitably, that all, regardless of national origin or status, might benefit.

Incentives would then be built, not on what a person has but on who they are and what they can contribute to the welfare of all. This would then set the stage for a system of core values upon which the humanity of the future would build its new foundation.

Cooperation rather than competition would be integrated into every aspect of life and would serve as the basis of all commerce and entertainment. Whether national pride, military might, or in the common everyday affairs of life, "winners and losers" would no longer be accepted as the norm.

Every person, regardless of race or their place in society, would be recognized for who they are and the potential they have for making a difference in the lives of others. No longer would there be the haves and the have-nots, the extremely rich and the extremely poor. All would be seen as they were born to be, honored members of the human family with attributes and abilities that contribute to the lives of all.

These are the possibilities for our children and future generations; a new world where the potential and gifts given to each is recognized and realized through mutual understanding and commitment to the sacredness and connectedness of all life.

This new world would be established not on monetary gain but on resources and interests shared by all, and opportunities provided to all, a world in which no member of the human family could "fail to succeed."

Who we are can only be measured from the inside out, not outside in.

In Search of Innocence

To find our way back to a place of innocence, to escape if but for a moment the disciplined, risk-free structures of our modern society where life has become one of struggle and survival, is a desire shared by all.

Every day and from every direction come a thousand and one voices telling us what to do and how to live, but only one that really matters; the still, small voice within. Somehow, we must find rest, some time away from it all, where our spirits can be renewed and strengthened for the day.

Though difficult given our intense schedules, when time is taken away from the stress we face almost every day, something rather extraordinary takes place. Our lives become more centered. In a sense, we become children again, trusting in a power greater than ourselves to guide and provide. There's a gradual movement away from distractions that slow us down. Anxiety and fear begin to lose their hold. The illusions that see life as adversary give way to the wonder of life as friend.

Time apart provides the opportunity for us to begin again. Every day becomes a new day. A sense of oneness to all that exists replaces feelings of isolation. Our return to the day's activities, no matter how challenging, has a new feel to it. Gradually we begin to see things differently. No longer is the mundane and accepted enough. Limitations our families and societies have placed upon us begin to fade, replaced by new possibilities.

When time is taken away from the required or routine, and our minds are brought back into harmony with the Source of everything, feelings of separation begin to fade, replaced with a sense of identity and closeness to life and everything life brings our way.

Life looks different now. A new perspective replaces the old paradigm. Struggle and despair give way to faith and trust. Appreciation for life and all it has to offer replaces anxiety about the past or fear of the future. Freed from the illusions of our minds and the restraints we carry, a new day begins to dawn, and with it, a new relationship to life begins.

> *As we learn to live more fully in the moment, anxiety about the hereafter will no longer be of great concern.*

The Silent Treatment

Though progress was slow and modern conveniences few, the "good ole days" may have had more to offer than we think. Time was a friend back then. Life unfolded naturally, and time helped dreams come true. But things have changed since then. Rather than moving us gently along at a pace we can manage, time appears to have taken over. We feel driven, controlled by its presence. As days go by and our responsibilities and commitments increase - families to care for, children to educate, professions to build – at times, we feel overwhelmed. Opportunities to be ourselves, to flow with the process, to be creative seem more limited now than ever.

Every day, in a thousand different ways, voices offer solutions to our dilemmas. Most, however, mislead, and the rest are temporary at best. Like those before us, we search for meaning, for answers in a world that requires much but leaves much to be desired.

Though it's true, an active life is often a long life, without some space, a quiet place away from the intensity of it all, the purpose of life begins to fade, replaced by patterns of behavior that more often than not have little meaning. By taking time to enter the stillness, we become more aware of ourselves, of others, and of the world around us. Feelings of separation and aloneness fade, replaced by a sense of connectedness. Like some great composition, our lives are brought back into harmony with the heartbeat of the universe, tuned to the rhythms of space and time. The creative spirit within is re-energized and becomes conscious of new opportunities, new adventures, new horizons to conquer.

In the silence, our vision becomes clearer, for we discover resources we never knew were there. Feelings of anxiety and fear fade, and a renewed sense of self begins to take shape. Our lives become more focused, more organized. We begin to see things from a different perspective. Insights into "what can be" replace feelings of frustration and despair. The restraints and limitations placed upon us by our families, friends, and societies are replaced by a sense of self-assurance and independence. Gradually we come to understand that we are more than we've been told, more than just reflections of people's ideas about us, that our greatest gift to ourselves and to the world is to be exactly who we are.

Time apart beyond the noise and activities of the day is never wasted. When we slow down and take "time off," life too slows down, and the results are predictable. Our ability to cope with daily challenges becomes greater, and our sense of self and what that means in relationship to others becomes clearer. Suddenly life looks different. Limitations become illusions, and new possibilities become a reality. Old habits give way to new patterns of living. No longer do we feel driven, controlled by circumstances, or out-of-control schedules. Once again, we are brought into harmony with the natural cycles and rhythm of the universe. Once again, time becomes a friend.

We must take time to rest if we expect to be fully awake.

Detours

The journey in life is never in a straight line. There are hills and valleys, sharp bends, narrow bridges, and even those unexpected detours.

It's inevitable. Just when you're making good time, or at least think you are, there's a detour, a bridge under construction, potholes to be filled, or a road needing to be resurfaced. Before you know it, you're miles out of the way on a narrow gravel road heading towards "outer Mongolia" or other parts unknown, rarely seen, much less inhabited by members of the human race.

Detours! We don't like them. They annoy us. They're inconvenient. They slow us down, move us in directions unfamiliar and sometimes a bit unnerving, but they do serve a purpose, perhaps more than we realize.

To continue along a chosen route and ignore construction site barriers or other warnings when a detour is indicated not only jeopardizes our means of transportation but could compromise life itself. To do so is extremely dangerous..

Life's detours may not be what we want, but they might be what we need. Who knows what beauty lies beyond the route of choice. Who knows what providence has in store when we are moved to change course, follow a new path, or go in a new direction.

Who knows …

Possibilities Unlimited

Although technology has advanced far beyond anything we or our ancestors could ever have imagined, it too has its limitations. We can use it to find our way to almost any destination with little risk of getting lost. No matter how sophisticated, however, it has little influence on the direction our lives take.

Whether we realize it or not, all of us are shaped by the culture and countries in which we are born. There are no exceptions. Our thoughts, relationships, and even our careers are conditioned by certain social norms, family customs, and religious or non-religious influences. We are the products of our environment, taught to live within certain boundaries, to walk the paths of our ancestors, and to build upon the ethics and insight of those who have gone before.

Even though our backgrounds influence the paths we take, they need not control our lives or limit our ability to make decisions unless we allow them to. Each of us is on a journey, exploring the unknown, trying to find ourselves in the midst of a world where the obsessive and abnormal are often more the norm than the exception.

Within each moment are opportunities to choose. We can live purposely or in a dreamlike state, allowing life to slip by with little awareness of who we are or where we're going, alive but not really living.

To drift along, swayed by the masses or the rhetoric of the day, may give us acceptance in some circles and an appearance of success, but it will never provide direction or the understanding we need to bring meaning to our lives.

Each of us can make a difference for ourselves and others if we choose to. To live with purpose, sensing our connectedness to all of life, consciously embracing and respecting life in whatever form it presents itself, gives depth and meaning to our lives far beyond our present reality.

As we experience anew the potential within and the unity of spirit that we all share, we will become like pioneers of old, exploring the unknown and creating opportunities for all in a new world of unlimited possibilities.

> *It's the struggles, the reaching out beyond ourselves that makes us who we are.*

> *How well off we are is not as important as how well off we leave others.*

On Becoming a Child

How was it when you were a child? Were you loved? Did you feel secure … safe? Was it okay just to be you?

For some, childhood brings memories of adventure, gentleness, acceptance, and understanding. For others, abuse, neglect, a sense of lostness. For most, a mixture; some memories good, and others rather sad.

Whatever it was like, maybe it's time to revisit those early years, explore again the magic and wonder of childhood, even recreate it if we wish.

To be truly mature, we must have the spirit of a child, a spirit that is open to discovery and creation, that celebrates and embraces all life brings our way.

Childlikeness. What a gift! Have you tried it on lately? When was the last time you chased a butterfly or a rainbow, climbed a tree or a mountain, or at least tried; ran through the rain or someone's sprinkler system, stood in awe in the presence of new life, or was touched by the beauty of a glorious sunset? How long has it been since you kissed a kitten, talked to a duck, or blew bubbles with a baby? When was the last time you made castles in the sand, hugged a bunny, or held a hand? How long has it been since you rose with the dawn, walked through a forest, or were surprised by a fawn?

To know again the laughter and joy of innocence. To look with wonder at the fantastic gifts life has to offer takes the mind and heart of a child. To live otherwise is not to live at all but merely exist. And what's the sense in life anyway if you can't be a child?

The soul flies on the wings of praise.

A Journey Through Time

Though silent, the hands of time move on at a relentless pace. Days become years. Summers turn to Fall. Winters to Spring. Regardless of our wishes or demands, time allows no shortcuts and has no favorites. To each, a moment is given, and within each moment, we define ourselves by the decisions we make.

As the seasons change, so do our stories; stories of love and loss, success and failure. Each journey is unique, an expression of who we are, moving us ever closer to our destinies. Circumstances may vary. Heredity and culture may have a voice, but we make the decisions, chart the course, create the future.

To each of us come moments of truth, decisions made that turn us around or move us in new directions. There are the many "hellos" that brighten our lives and the sad "goodbyes" that help us grow. There's joy and laughter, but times too when our hearts are heavy and our minds clouded with pain or sadness.

We may never accomplish all we would like or experience all there is to experience, for time has boundaries, but we can live a life that is full and complete if we wish. Our investment in life is a good one, no matter where our journeys take us or how challenging the way.

A Word to The Wise

Words. Though limited at best and frequently misunderstood, words are used to express our thoughts and feelings. It's how we connect to one another, at least most the time.

Words and expressions come at us from every direction, building us up, tearing us down. They inspire. They limit. Their power and influence invade every corner of our lives. Without them, communication would be difficult though not impossible. Could it be there might be other ways to connect we may not yet be aware of?

Though few remember, understandably so, our journeys in this world began without words, for there weren't any. Somehow though, our needs were made known to our parents and others who cared for us.

We may not realize it, but we are all part of a system of communication more sophisticated and complex than anything in our world of advanced technology. Though appearances may deceive, nothing in creation is isolated or alone. Everything is connected to everything else through networks and at frequencies that are constant and ongoing. This interconnectedness recognizes and responds to the needs of all.

Could it be that our species, like other forms of life in the universe, can communicate on levels even more profound and complete than our current system?

Whether accurate or not, there are those that reference a time in human history when we, too, knew how to express ourselves in ways beyond words. Is it possible that we might someday "return" to this higher form of communication?

In today's world, our means of connecting with each other has reached a level that would have appeared mysterious, even magical, to our ancestors. We are amazed at the tremendous advances science and technology have made. What is said in one corner of the world can be "heard" anywhere in any part of the world at any time.

If we humans can create sophisticated methods of communication, is it not possible the Power behind creation is capable of communicating directly with that which he has created both here and beyond? Could it be there are unused powers and potential lying dormant within that we have yet to discover?

Perhaps the time will come when the human race will rediscover the creative power and potential of the human spirit, a power that allows us to express ourselves and be understood in ways beyond the norm of today.

In order for us to experience this advanced level of communication, however, we must break through the illusion that we are separate from one another or anything else for that matter. We must embrace the reality of our connectedness to all life in whatever form it appears, for the life force that has brought all that is into existence is the ultimate source and channel of all true communication.

When we enter this new phase of our journey, when we see our true identity, that nothing is separate from anything, that we are all one, a new phase in human communication and cooperation will open before us, far more advanced than anything we know today.

*When the heart speaks,
words are not necessary.*

The Journey

Whether at home or abroad, each of us is on a journey, embracing the old, exploring the new, continually shaped by the experiences we go through. We're never the same, nor are the traditions and cultures of which we are a part. Everything is evolving. changing, becoming. At every turn, wherever we are, whatever the circumstances, life comes to us from all directions, continually moving us from the familiar to the unknown.

Because the evolving process is subtle and slow, we may not be conscious of how much change has taken place over time, but it has. Nothing stays the same … ever! Life creates life. It never comes to a standstill, nor would we want it to.

We are human "beings," but exactly what we will "be" today or tomorrow is yet "to be." Much is determined by how we relate to the experiences and people who enter our lives and the lives we enter, the decisions we make when we prosper or face adversity. Each moment provides us with opportunities to move beyond the limitations placed upon us by ourselves or others' past or present.

We are far more than we realize. To marginalize our gifts, to be satisfied with less than who we really are, is not only a disservice to ourselves but to those around us who are awaiting our presence. As our consciousness and connectedness to life increase, we will understand more clearly our place and purpose in the world. Opportunities will present themselves that not only change our lives but also affect others.

If we are conscious and awake to the needs and suffering around us, life will appear to us in ways we have not known before. On every street corner, around every bend, we will see them; faces pleading, hearts crying for someone to listen, to care, to free them from the despair and aloneness that has taken over their lives.

Could it be we, too, experience healing when we respond to the needs of others? Could it be our efforts to release them from their fears and despair releases us from ours as well? When we understand the journey we are on is a shared experience, and that what we do for others, we do for ourselves, a new dimension in living will open before us, and life will reveal itself to us in ways we can only now begin to imagine.

Accepting the Unacceptable

No matter how well off or how exemplary a life, all of us must face life on its terms. There are no exemptions or exceptions. Though we may think otherwise, trying to protect ourselves, our loved ones, or our friends from the unpleasant or unwanted may not be in their best interest or ours.

Though the scenery on this shared adventure is beautiful, there are dangers along the way and more than enough detours.

We may not always like what the Hand of Providence allows or how it affects those close to us, but there are times when we must accept the unacceptable, knowing that somehow the One who has brought life into being can bring about the best in any situation no matter how intimidating or how difficult.

The Awakening

To suddenly enter a new dimension after having all our needs cared for is not something we would wish on anyone, yet all of us have had this experience. Surrounded by lights and strange noises, we came into the world with no idea who we were or where we were. All we knew was we were here, wherever that was.

Although nothing came with us, nor could we identify anything, the journey had begun, an adventure into the unknown. We were explorers on a mission ... to somewhere.

Though the process was slow, our understanding of who we were gradually became clearer. At a deeper level, we realized there was a reason for our entry into the world, much more profound than the mythology of our cultural stories or the messages of our modern world.

Over time our sense of self evolved. We began to see things from a different perspective. Though not without struggle, our attraction to the external gradually began to fade, and the intangible yet real slowly took its place.

The restraints and limitations imposed upon us began to give way to new ways of thinking and living. No longer were we bound by people or circumstances nor controlled by those in positions of power. Our place in the world and the meaning of existence become clearer. We now understood that our lives extended beyond the temporary.

As we grew and became more conscious of our divine heritage and our connection to all, fear began to lose its power. We now knew we were exactly where we were meant to be. The timing and place of our entry into the world were not by accident or coincidence.

Though, unfortunately, few experience change at this level, the opportunity is open to all. To live consciously; fully awake to the present moment is to know life at a depth and dimension beyond the ordinary. When we understand our true nature and who we really are, feelings of aloneness and isolation will fade, replaced by a sense of connection to life in whatever form it appears.

This is the life we were meant to live, and when embraced will transform the human race. A new era will then begin. Heaven will touch earth, and peace on earth good will toward men will no longer be a desire but a reality.

Hope

Life comes to us in ways far different than we expect. Rarely does it follow the path our minds imagine, nor should it. Conditioned by family and cultural traditions, our understanding of what life is all about is more a reflection of what others think and expect than what reality presents.

Life can be challenging and often is, but it was never meant to be more than we could handle. No matter how steep the climb or how difficult the way, when we understand the divine plan behind this experience called life, we will know all things, even the worst imaginable, work in our best interest. Regardless of what we face, life can be and should be an experience of joy, a never-ending adventure into the unknown with new horizons just ahead and new heights to be reached.

Progress, not perfection, is what the journey is about. It's the good times and not-so-good that bring us the experiences we need and remind us of what's really of value.

Are there regrets? Missed opportunities? Of course. Who hasn't missed the mark, fallen from the path, spoken unwisely, hurt others, or yielded to temptation? None are perfect, but we're all special. All of us are evolving, changing, becoming. Life is a process, not a destination.

Patience with ourselves and others is what is needed. We are all children learning to walk. We stumble, fall, then struggle to get up. Shame and guilt keep us down, but a hand that cares, and a heart that understands, gives us the courage to try again.

When shadows gather and darkness surrounds, it may appear we are forgotten or forsaken, but this is not true. We are never forsaken or alone. The whole universe is on our side. The very Source of all that exists is there to see us through even the most difficult experiences. When we awaken to our own potential and the possibilities life has to offer, struggles will be a thing of the past. Life will be embraced as the gift it was always meant to be. Hope will no longer be an illusion but a reality.

> God's heart and God's love are as big as the universe. No one nor anything is ever excluded.

The Spirit of Who We Are

What does it mean to be spiritual? Is that the same as being religious? Can a person be spiritual and not religious or religious and not spiritual?

Although the nature of spirituality is difficult to define, it seems to be at the very center of who we are as human beings. Though mysterious, its creative force can be felt throughout the world of nature, from the tiniest microcosm to spaces so vast even measurements at the speed of light seem inadequate.

Could it be spirituality has more to do with who we are than what we believe? Could it be that what we hold in our hearts is just as important as the tenets and doctrines we uphold from our respective religious traditions?

Spirituality is not a commodity, some product we buy or inherit. It's not a possession. In a sense, it's an attitude, a condition, a state of mind and heart. It's a desire from deep within to find strength and meaning in life ... to be all we were meant to be.

In a way it's a movement toward health and wholeness, a restorative process by which healing takes place within ourselves, in our relationship to God, to others, and to life itself.

To be truly connected in a personal, intimate way to the great Creator of all and to the world around us, continually growing and evolving in our sense of joy at the works and wonders of creation, may have more to do with true spirituality than we think.

To carry this spirit within our hearts each day provides a center for living that will see us through even the most difficult experiences. In time it will bring us a sense of serenity and spiritual balance that will help keep us on track no matter where we are along the journey called "life."

🕊 A religion of the mind needs requirements; that of the spirit needs nothing.

Commitment

It takes courage to face the difficult experiences in life, the unexpected that throw us off balance or move us in new directions. Though we may not understand why we face certain conditions or experiences, all are gifts. True. Some we would just as soon do without, but all have a purpose and, if accepted, in time, work in our best interest.

Although by definition, gifts are free, in a sense, they do cost. An investment is required. A commitment. We can have, be, or do whatever we wish. Freedom of choice is ours. But along with freedom comes responsibility. Choosing responsibly means following through with our choices. Without commitment, the goals we choose in life, personal or professional, mean little. They're only dreams ... empty, lifeless dreams.

Dreams, however, do come true, but only when they become more than just wishful thinking.

To wish for a thing is commendable. To hope for something is admirable. To actually commit to something, now that is creative.

It's the struggles, the reaching out beyond ourselves that move us to new heights and new experiences.

The Shadow Side of the Beautiful

Whether stained-glass windows or elaborate mosaics, it's the shadows, the dark contours, the gray subtleties that bring out the richness of color or design the artist had in mind.

So too, is the story of our lives. Often when least expected clouds gather, and we go through experiences, we'd rather not. Health problems, economic loss, dreams put on hold or destroyed, relationships gone awry. Without warning, our lives turn inside out or upside down, like paper boats bouncing around in a Pacific storm.

The "why's" come easy but not the answers. We live within the mystery of life and the complexities of the human experience. To each of us come times of stress and disappointment. No one escapes.

Though our understanding is limited, the Master Artist, unseen and often unrecognized, bends over the easel of our lives, slowly, patiently bringing out the rich colors and uniqueness of each of his creations for all are works of art.

To be patient with the process, to accept circumstances and conditions we may not completely understand allows the Master Artist freedom to do His best work. And since His abilities are far greater than ours, the finished product, with its shadows and special effects, is always perfect.

Standing Together

Even though "getting away from it all" can be helpful, we also need time together. Life lived in a vacuum is not only difficult; it's impossible. Barriers erected to keep the world away can easily become walls that isolate.

Regardless of who we are or what our backgrounds, we hold much in common. We're human, part of the same family. Our loves and losses, concerns and challenges remind us of how much we need each other.

Each day gives us opportunities to love and be loved, to find strength through the kindness and compassion of others.

As we move beyond the safety and comfort of the known to touch the lives of those around us, concerning ourselves with their concerns, our lives too will be changed. No matter how difficult the circumstances, when we understand ours is a shared journey, that we're here to support each other, we will experience a new level of healing not only personally but in all our relationships.

❧ The physical may bring us together, but only love can keep us together.

It's Friday!

It may not hit the top ten, but the tune's familiar. In fact, it's become the theme song of a rather large group. Old and young alike, professional and non, have joined the chorus. Some sing it with enthusiasm, others rather quietly, but whether sung with a sigh, a shout, or a cry, it still sounds the same, "Thank God, it's Friday!"

How come this "song" is so popular? What's behind the frustration, the fears, the struggles? Could it be we're a bit off course, missed a turn somewhere?

We speak proudly of the tremendous progress our society has made, but have we really? We possess more and have less. Our world has become smaller, and so have we. We move faster than ever, yet seem to be getting farther and farther behind. We have more to do and less time. We champion the cause of freedom and are more limited, more restricted today than ever.

Was life really meant to be this difficult, this challenging? Is there nothing to hold on to? Are we, as some would suggest, adrift in a cold and hostile universe, or is it just our perspectives that are a bit off balance?

Perhaps we need to back up a little and reassess what this journey is all about; take a second look at the messages and messengers who've tried to shape our lives in ways that don't work. Maybe we need to slow down a bit, get in touch with our thoughts and feelings rather than allowing others to tell us who we are and what's important.

If, in our rush to enter the day, we would allow time and ourselves to stand still, spend time in the silence, we might rediscover something very important – ourselves! And with that discovery, it's very possible we might gain a better understanding and appreciation for each moment and those relationships that bring meaning to our lives. In fact, one never knows if we keep it up, the day may come when we'll have a new theme song, "Thank God, it's Monday! "

No matter the circumstances, when time is taken for communion with the Divine, peace and rest will be ours regardless of what's happening around us.

Love

Like the ocean of air around us, love is invisible. We can feel it, enjoy it, even get a real high out of it, or when the weather gets a bit stormy, we can get frightened or even hurt by it.

We know when it's present. We know when it's not, but to actually see it – oh no! We can only experience it.

Musicians, poets, writers, theologians, both ancient and modern, have tried their hand at defining love. Their insights are helpful but never complete. Love as a subject, emotion, or experience has no boundaries except as we create them.

Like a golden thread, love weaves itself in and out of every experience we go through. Its power and influence encompass the entire spectrum of life. From our first cry 'till the day we die, its presence changes, rearranges, and transforms us into a thing of beauty if we allow it to do so, like an artist patiently chipping away at a block of stone, soon to become a work of art.

Though definitions may elude us, we can each experience the mystery and wonder of love. In fact, we must! Without God, without love, life is not lived. It's just endured.

> *Love needs no recognition or response. It can only be experienced and shared.*

Time Out

Though at times intense and a bit overwhelming, the journey in life is quite an adventure. Regardless of position or profession, not many, if any, escape life's pressures and demands.

With few exceptions, the desire to get things done takes priority. Our "to-do" lists seem endless. In our intense drive to succeed, we often find ourselves out of step with what's really important.

Could it be we need "time out," some place or space away from it all, where nothing is all there is and silence alone has a voice?

Perhaps a break now and then, a few moments to refocus the heart and spirit, is what is needed. The truth is, without time apart, sooner or later we "fall apart."

To neglect the inner life is costly. If we don't take time to go within, we will ultimately go ... without.

Use your time wisely; otherwise it will be a very poor investment.

Seeing is Believing, Or Is It?

To accept life in whatever way it presents itself takes courage, especially when the undesirable shows up and what we want doesn't. To live life within the space of our desires, our wants and the reality of what is, can at times be frustrating, sometimes discouraging, but may also be what we need.

Our backgrounds shape our beliefs and how we live more than we realize. What we see around us or imagine we see is used to build the foundation upon which our lives are built. Our perceptions create the game of life, and our beliefs create the rules.

But perceptions and beliefs are not ultimate reality. They are only reflections of the real, some reliable and some not. Often what we see or think we see is but a shadow of what is real.

Could it be that what we have learned from our friends, our families, even our traditions is just another way of looking at things? Is it possible the "game of life" can be played in more than one way?

The truth is we don't know it all. In fact, we don't know much at all. To be open to questions still to be asked and answers that could change the way we see things is not only possible but probable.

Like the rays of a glorious sunrise, the landscapes of our lives are continually changing. Patterns of light etched in time are creating tapestries of beauty beyond description. As the moments pass and the scenes change, life presents itself in a thousand different ways, each special, each unique and each meant to open up new horizons, new adventures for us to explore.

To accept the known for what it is, a reflection of the unknown still to be explored is a wisdom that will move us to a life lived beyond our wildest dreams, a journey of discovery both temporal and eternal.

♆ Love sees the best in the worst and perfection in that which appears imperfect.

Life Without Limits

Life is not so much a journey of the mind as it is of the heart. It's a process, an adventure of discovery, and the greatest discovery of all are the treasures within.

Though we may have forgotten, we are all rich. This is how we came into the world. It's our inheritance.

Like an undiscovered bank account, all the resources and power of the universe are at our disposal, but unless or until we "remember" that such an account exists, it might as well not be, for it serves no purpose. Once "discovered," however, we can withdraw whatever amounts we wish to be used in whatever ways we choose.

To have access to unlimited resources takes away the restrictions we so often place upon ourselves. The "sky's the limit" no longer applies. There are no limits. When we know what's there and who it is that backs us up, we'll be able to do, be or have whatever we choose.

To live life without limits is exciting. There are all sorts of possibilities. Who knows what we might become, might accomplish or what lives we might touch. Nothing is beyond our reach. Nothing can hold us back when we realize how really well-off we are.

Come close – go far.

Happiness is ...

Happiness is a choice. Sounds strange, doesn't it? But it's true. Happiness IS a choice. It's not some magical experience that unexpectedly "happens" to us somewhere along the way, nor is it determined by where we live or the family we were born into.

As children and even as adults, we imagine a life that arranges itself in line with our needs or desires, but things don't always work out according to our plans. In fact, seldom do they, nor do others always agree with our wishes or demands.

We may have some great relationships, but there will also be times of disagreement and disappointment. Listening to others who care is wise, but allowing their opinions to control how we live and the decisions we make is not.

Life happens the way it happens, and it's up to us to decide how to relate to the experiences we go through. If we see circumstances or events as undermining or offensive, our happiness will disappear like mist before the morning sun.

All of us must make choices. We can fight or accept what comes our way, become better or bitter. It's up to us. By resisting or fighting "what is," we disempower ourselves for "what is ... IS." and there's nothing we can do about it. It's already here. It's already happened. Our job is not to try and change whatever's occurred (that would be impossible) but to accept.

Although we may not be consciously aware, on some level, we call to ourselves people and situations that help move us from who we think we are to who we really are and where we need to be. We begin to understand a universal truth. Life doesn't happen "to us" but "through us." This process is gradual, ongoing, and constant. How we relate to what we go through is directly related to our understanding of life and the meaning of existence.

When we embrace the darkness as well as the light, when we see the gift in every experience, regardless of how those gifts arrive, we will know that all things do work together for our good. It is then, regardless of how difficult or challenging, happiness will no longer be a fleeting experience, determined by whim or circumstance or the opinions and actions of others, but will always - all ways - be a choice.

- *Happiness comes from accepting whatever comes our way, not everything going our way.*

- *Happiness is a choice, not an experience.*

Imperfectly Perfect

Whether we realize it or not, our backgrounds play a very important part on how we live. Unfortunately, many of the messages we receive affect us in ways that do more harm than good. Though expected and accepted, they are often out of touch with reality and compromise not only the innocence and integrity of childhood but also marginalize the ability of adults to reach their full potential.

Life is not lived in a vacuum. It's a gradual and often painful process, an awakening of the spirit within, a learning and remembering that takes a lifetime. It's a journey, not an overnight experience. To believe somewhere along the way, we'll eventually reach a state of perfection is an illusion, yet this illusion in one form or another is embraced by many.

Parents want their children to be perfect and children their parents. Communities expect perfection of their governments and leadership. Parishioners want their pastors and priests to be perfect and look forward to a perfect world to come. Educational systems reward students whose academic performance is near perfect. Organizations and companies across the world concerned about their image honor employees whose work meets certain standards of perfection.

With few exceptions, we too get caught up in the desire to be perfect, especially critical of ourselves when we don't measure up, don't say or do the right thing, when our actions or appearance betray us, or when others don't reach the standard of perfection, we expect.

Is it possible, however, in the grand scheme of things, perfection is not what we think it is? Could it be the forces at work that shape the experiences we go through are exactly what are needed? Is it possible the universe defines perfection differently than we do?

To the untrained eye, creation leaves much to be desired. It seems disorganized; incomplete. Mountain ranges with summits reaching far above the plains are rugged and uneven. Flowers spread across a million fields appear scattered and disconnected. Trees with branches uneven, twisted, and bent cover the landscape. Nature seems to be unsure of itself, a product of uncertainty and confusion, yet in and through it all, the Unseen seems satisfied with its completeness, its perfection just the way it is.

At times our lives too leave much to be desired. The unexpected enters our lives, and we don't know what to do or which way to turn. Unwise choices turn us away from our dreams and lead us down paths that go nowhere. Hereditary weaknesses, out-of-control addictions, and challenges that seem to come from nowhere weaken our ability to face the difficult and unexpected.

Like the natural world around us, our lives, too, seem uncertain and incomplete. The unforeseen and unwanted weave themselves in and out of our lives seemingly at will. Financial challenges, health issues, relationships gone awry throw us off balance or worse.

Overwhelmed by conditions that defy our greatest efforts, we wonder what it's all about and why things are not going the way we want. If, however, we could see the end from the beginning, we would realize, no matter how difficult ... everything *IS* going the way it should and ultimately everything will work out for our good as well as for those around us.

We are like children learning to walk. We stumble, we fall, but get up and try again and again. To the soul, there is no such thing as failure; every trying is a success. There are no mistakes, only lessons to be learned. Our progress in life is not measured by how many times we fall but how many times we get up. It's the getting up, the decisions we make in each moment of now however small, that limits us or open up possibilities for a greater, grander future.

Though some may think otherwise, our journey in this world is not the result of fate, some random venture that destiny has prearranged, nor is it a destination. The universe provides opportunities to turn what we know about ourselves into experience. It's an adventure in time, a process, an ever-changing experience of learning and unlearning, of forgetting and remembering.

Unlike ultimate reality, we were born into a universe of contrasts, of opposites, a created environment of beginnings and endings within the boundaries of time. Like the changing seasons, it is only in this field of contrasts, of opposites – of good and bad, light and darkness, love and fear - that we have the power of choice, otherwise there would be no choice at all for there would be nothing to choose from.

Relationships to everything and everyone are what life is all about, not only personal relationships – men and women to each other, parents to children, children to children, friends with friends – but also the decisions we make when the unexpected comes our way – natural disasters, accidents, health issues, physical or emotional loss - and the many other experiences we go through, the results of which, given our choices, make us less than who we are or far greater than we could imagine.

The paths we take are often rugged and unfamiliar, yet they bring us exactly what we need, perfectly timed and perfectly suited to each, regardless of our backgrounds.

Though defined differently than reason or logic allow, in truth there is no such thing as imperfection. It only exists in our minds. Regardless of appearances or the decisions made personally or collectively that bring about certain results, the universe, from the infinitely small to light years of incomprehensible grandness, is absolutely perfect. It can be no other way for all that is and ever has been is but a reflection in physical form of that perfect creative power that brought all that is into existence.

Like the moving parts of some intricate piece of machinery or the texture and colors in a magnificent work of art, so too is this cosmic experience we are all involved in. Each of us is playing a part, none less or more important than another ... actors in a universal, absolutely perfect production that had its beginnings in eternity and will continue throughout all the forever's yet to come.

Our lives are perfectly imperfect and perfectly suited to each person's life experience.

Another Look at Love

How does one describe the indescribable or measure that which cannot be measured? How does one take the creative energy, the very source of all that exists, and put it into words?

It's not possible. It can't be done, and that's just the way it is. The best we can do is share what we see at the moment and let that be enough, one small drop of understanding in an infinite ocean of truth.

That's how it is when we talk about love. It's magical! It's mysterious, and it defies all attempts to define it. It's as big as the universe, greater than anything we could ever imagine, and far deeper than any philosopher or wise man could ever conceive.

Love goes beyond language. It's an energy that is felt and experienced. It takes sadness and turns it into joy. It makes the most difficult bearable and creates brightness and beauty where once was darkness and despair.

When expressed from the heart, love has no limits. It crosses all boundaries, all traditions and transforms all who come under its influence. Whatever it embraces, it makes whole. Its language is universal; it's power and influences eternal.

> ✣ *Nothing in our best interest consistent with love is ever kept from us.*

The Challenge of Change

Though it's natural to try and hold on to the familiar, seldom does life allow us to remain where we are. Throughout our lives, we are constantly challenged by forces that manage and create new experiences. Summers turn to fall, winters to spring. A child is born. There's a new beginning, a new life.

Regardless of our desires or demands, life expresses itself in ways that are constant yet everchanging, an ongoing process bounded by time yet eternal in nature.

Acceptance of the present, no matter how it appears, transforms our lives and prepares us for new adventures. It takes the fear out of living and replaces it with an understanding that ultimately, whatever we face will not only be to our benefit but to those around us as well.

Life is full of surprises and rewards those who are willing to accept it on its terms. Interruptions that disturb may not be what we want but could be what we need.

Whether expected or not, around every corner and in every moment, our lives are challenged by change. If allowed, an acceptance of this process will provide us opportunities to move in new directions, to experience life in ways far beyond our imagined limitations.

The Ideal and the Real

No matter what possibilities lie ahead, there is no such thing as independence at birth. Basic needs for all early on are cared for by others. Over time however, though each path is different, all awaken to a much bigger world.

Childhood interests are eventually left behind replaced by new ways of thinking, new ways of living. Cultural traditions and family expectations are reexamined. Even religious preferences may be seen differently through eyes that are now more mature. Knowledge is still important, but wisdom and insight appear of more value as does intuition over intellect.

The journey is not the same now nor are we. Old concepts give way to new paradigms. No longer do we see ourselves apart from but a part of all that exists. There is a shift in how we define ourselves, our relationships and life in general, almost like a rebirth experience. Consciousness not only changes our view of the universe but redefines the meaning of existence. Systems of logic meant to regulate life are no longer seen as the final word on our preferences or the directions our lives take. We are on a journey to nowhere and everywhere and the decisions we make are our own.

This transition to a higher level of consciousness, brings to mind a great truth, that no matter who we are or where we come from, the origins of all are the same. We share a common heritage. Nothing is separate from anything and never has been. Every man is my brother, every woman my sister and all children are mine. This awakening reminds us that whatever we do or don't do that undermines or destroys another or any part of creation is also putting ourselves at risk.

As the journey continues, religious beliefs, traditional customs, or political ideals upon which we once based many of our decisions also begin to change. Systems of thought and organizations upon which we often relied for guidance no longer have power over us as they once did, nor are they allowed the final word on how we live or express ourselves.

Although this awakening experience gives us a new perspective on life, it does not mean we always live in ways consistent with truths we now understand. In the world we have created, where the spiritual is marginalized, technology prioritized and relationships discounted, it's easy to get off course, lost in a wilderness of illusions and expectations that move us in directions inconsistent with who we are.

When life gets in the way of what we expect, even the best of us can lose our way. Wants turned to needs conditioned by outside influences can cause the mind to embrace the imagined in place of the real, gradually moving us away from where we should be into a fantasy land of expectations. Life no longer unfolds as it was meant to but is now seen as servant to our wishes and demands rather than a process that encourages growth and change.

Expectations. Our lists are long and with few exceptions play a significant role in our relationships. Colleagues, friends and those closest to us are expected to respond according to certain requirements our minds have put in place. None escape, including our children; their lives meant to be a reflection of what they've been taught even if their teachers are not.

No matter how long our lists, they are never complete without including a close acquaintance of whom we are extremely critical and that's the person we see in the mirror each morning. The way we treat ourselves when we don't quite measure up is often far more intense than any criticism or treatment by others.

Though reluctant to express our thoughts, in a sense our expectations go far beyond the "here and now" and are really a form of judgement not only of ourselves and life in general but of the One who created life. Though subtle, we've been told or brought to believe that life is supposed to bend to what we feel is best, consistent with our beliefs and behavior and when it doesn't, not only do we blame ourselves but we begin to question the motives and integrity of the power behind existence. Since we are held accountable for our words and actions, shouldn't he be held accountable as well for his apparent inconsistency in how he responds to his children, that is if he responds at all?

We wonder. Is it possible the One who created our ability to see and hear is blind to the struggles we face, deaf to our cries for help? Even though we do our best, where is he when we need him most, when things fall apart? Why is it at times we feel so alone, so forgotten, so forsaken? Is there not some oasis somewhere where faith and trust are recognized ... honored ... restored?

Most of us are aware of an historical figure called "doubting Thomas." What we might not know, however, is that he is still alive and well. He lives inside each of us and makes his presence known at almost every turn of our journey. Because our understanding of life is limited and our expectations of ourselves and God are misunderstood, we respond to the experiences we go though in ways that create doubt, frustration and anger.

When what we think we need is ignored or at least appears to be; when challenges appear around almost every corner, and even mother nature turns her back, we begin to question. We don't want others to know but there are times when we're not sure God really knows what he's doing. Why doesn't he intervene when evil has the upper hand, when innocent lives are lost, when the insane becomes the norm and our lives feel so out of balance? Why is it when we long for rest and at least some semblance of sanity and security, we end up bouncing around on a sea of uncertainty or marooned on a desolate island somewhere?

Could it be the Creator knows something we don't; that there is more to life than what we want or expect, that no matter how much we wish it were different, not everything is going to fall into place as we would like, that though we might think otherwise, God may not need our help after all? Is it possible our faith must give way to trust, that our desires to feel comfortable, in control and secure may not always be in our best interest nor a priority in the mind of God?

In the lives of all, even the greatest, are stretches of land, barren and desolate and rugged mountains to be conquered. Life is not a gentle downstream experience. Like the changing seasons or the waves of the sea, sometimes calm, sometimes not, life was meant to be experienced in ways often opposite what we want or expect.

Without exception storms will come. Our lives will be battered and torn by the elements and much we've held on to destroyed, but no matter what we go through, how intense or difficult, everything has its purpose in the mind of God.

The struggle to get through the desert; the strength and perseverance needed to reach the mountain top are all part of the process God has allowed in order to move us from who we think we are to the beings we are becoming.

We must experience the good, the bad and everything in between in order to understand the lessons life has to offer and the meaning of infinite unconditional love. Although unseen and often unrecognized he is never absent from that which he has created. There are no mistakes and nothing is coincidental in God's world.

Though from a divine perspective the ultimate outcome of life is never in doubt, from a human perspective anything close to perfection is extremely difficult for us to grasp. We are each very much aware of those times many of us – make that all of us – say things, do things, make decisions that we regret; times when our minds get in the way of our hearts and we end up on detours … shortcuts to nowhere. That's usually when the voices in our heads that got us into trouble in the first place, go into overtime, shouting expletives, reminding us in no uncertain terms how messed up we are.

The story could easily end here and unfortunately has for many, but for those who listen closely, beyond the noise in our heads, another voice, soft yet assuring, speaks to our minds and hearts. This voice coming from the silence within is the One who gave us life and who is ready when we are, to help us take the next step towards self-expression and self-discovery.

If we listen closely, he can be heard bringing comfort to our hearts and release from the false accusations of our minds reminding us of our unworthiness. He is the one who knows everything about us, far beyond those who are closest. He understands our weaknesses, knows our strengths and the longings of our hearts. He sees the potential, the abilities we've been given yet to be developed. If allowed, the hand that creates has the power to recreate and restore as he has done through the ages. No matter who we are, where we are or what we have done, no one is beyond hope ... ever.

To plan for the days ahead is fine, but to allow expectations to be the driving force behind our decisions takes us beyond reality into a land of wishful thinking, where unfortunately dreams at times become nightmares. It leaves little room for making decisions outside the limits of our minds. In a sense we limit God as well. We either see ourselves as too unimportant for God to notice or too unworthy of whatever it is he has in store. Though often used to put down or belittle, given where we are and where we'd like to be, perhaps it would be well to ask ourselves an age-old question ... "Who do you think you are?" The answer to that question will either keep us stuck in old patterns of behavior or allow us to embrace new concepts, new ways of living.

Though we have been taught otherwise, we must understand that each of us is unique, special. We are not reflections of what others have told us about ourselves nor is our identity attached to a particular ideal or profession. We are spiritual beings created in the mind of God given opportunities in the realm of the physical to create and experience life in ways that allow us to evolve to new levels of consciousness.

There may be times when we feel insignificant, marginalized but we are not. We are much more than we think we are, and even though our journeys in this world are extremely short compared to all the forevers of the past and those to come, our lives have tremendous value beyond what others have told us or the realities we have created. Our names, our faces, what we did, or how famous we were, may not be remembered but on some level the love and compassion we have shown and shared with others during our journey on earth will make a difference not only in the here and now, but in the lives of generations yet to come.

> *God is only limited in that he can only reveal himself to us along those paths with which we are familiar and only by how open we are to receive.*

Out of the Silence

Everything in creation is in motion, from the invisible to the largest galaxies in space. Nothing stands still. Life without some level of activity cannot exist. However, activity alone is not growth, nor is movement the same as progress.

Without purpose, dedication, and commitment have little meaning. So too, is success if we don't know what it means to succeed.

To find serenity and balance in a world where unrest is the norm is not easy. To be aware of the spirit within, in an atmosphere of surround sound and virtual reality, is not easy either. To do less, however, not only puts us at a disadvantage, it makes us incapable of being present for ourselves or others. Strength from within versus power from without keeps us connected and provides direction to our lives.

To experience life more fully, it must be explored more deeply. In the stillness lies tremendous power, silently, quietly expressing itself in the ongoing creation of life itself. Trees bud. Flowers bloom. Tides rise and fall. Dusk and dawn follow each other as they always have while the planet spins its way through the universe.

In the stillness the Creator is present, and there too we shall discover who we are. Out of the silence comes power to live, strength to become who we choose to be. Out of the silence the Divine takes on the human and the human is transformed by the Divine.

> *The Divine speaks to our hearts through the world of nature but cannot be heard until the world we have created is silenced.*

A Composition of the Ages

No matter how gifted or not, all of us play a part in the grand musical production of the ages. As to what instrument we choose or how well we perform is up to us.

Although backgrounds differ, we are each given opportunities to bring our lives into line with the rhythm of the universe, choosing in each moment whether to bring discord or harmony to the composition underway.

As in all great music, contrasts in style and tempo are meant to bring about certain feelings and responses. At times, like an eagle disappearing into the heights above, the music takes off, spiraling into space, creating a sense of magnificence and awe, then gently falling back to earth in slow, rhythmic patterns leaving a sense of gentleness and peace.

This production with its origins in the distant past, is composed of musicians throughout the universe, and presents a mixture of sound, colors, and textures that are a reflection of life itself. As the moments of forever evolve, its musical score changes, resonating to the frequency of time and space, bringing the richness of all creation into a composition of intricacy and beauty beyond description.

Although there are no soloists, all of us contribute and benefit from this grand musical masterpiece. Shared by all, this special opportunity and experience bring about a new understanding of life and our relationships to one another. If allowed, it will bring us together, keep us together, and will redefine our understanding of what it means to be a human family, each member of which is being brought back into harmony with the heartbeat of the universe.

❦ Care and compassion measure progress, not technology.

❦ The present is all there is. We cannot see a sunrise, feel the rain dance on our faces, or appreciate the beauty of a flower yesterday or tomorrow – only in the moment.

Reflections or Reality

To be mechanically inclined, informationally informed, and technologically advanced is a significant part of the mindset of our modern society. Effectiveness, competency, thoroughness, and productivity are the goals to be reached.

Ours is an age of the intellectually astute and organizationally efficient. We can analyze, systematize, organize, and categorize most anything. Together with our computers, we can create what formerly was unheard of, from multicolored charts and graphs and sophisticated data bases to Hollywood illusions that seem more real than reality. Through ingenuity and a willingness to explore the unknown, we have created a technological universe far in advance of anything our ancestors could ever have imagined.

An appreciation of our abilities to create is worthy of respect and even praise, but we must understand that no matter how wonderful or fantastic our inventions, they are not us. They are only reproductions, reflections of the creative potential of the human mind.

To become servants to our creations, to worship what our hands or minds have made is to make ourselves less than who we are. In so doing, we become shadows, reflections and if we're not careful ... slaves to our own technology.

Focusing on the external as individuals or organizations at the expense of the internal undermines that which gives our accomplishments meaning. Whether at work, at play, or in our day-to-day activities, all that we do is informed, deformed, or transformed by who we are, and who we are shapes what we do.

To neglect or ignore the creative elements of the human spirit that empower and make our achievements meaningful accomplishes little beyond the superficial. Without heart, without a vital connection to the inner life, our accomplishments are more illusion than reality.

Those who volunteer to correct the faults of others are often the ones in greatest need themselves.

We play our games as if they were real and treat the real as if they were games.

Your Attention Please

Although the decisions we make are not always the best, none of us come into the world empty-handed. Like the wise men of old, we come bearing gifts. In fact, each of us *IS* a gift. We were never meant to take this journey alone. It's a shared experience with gifts being exchanged all the time. In a sense, we need each other in order to know and be who we really are.

Unfortunately, there are times when decisions are made that compromise our abilities. We get distracted by thoughts and actions that sabotage our dreams.

Though subtle, every day through the media, internet and other means of communication, our senses are overloaded with ideas and suggestions that get us off course. They appear in forms, often disguised, that appeal to our minds or our sense of beauty but lead us down paths and through experiences that compromise our true worth and purpose in life.

Today our advantages over former generations are great. Technology has torn down the walls that separate us. We can communicate with anyone, anytime, anywhere in the world. Through virtual reality we can tap into the latest discoveries, explore the unknown, learn the latest from scientific research, keep up with our favorite sports, or move into realms of fantasy without ever leaving our homes.

Technology, however, and the resources it makes available, no matter how worthy, is never to our advantage when it depletes our energies, compromises our dreams, or diverts us onto paths that discount our greatest potential.

A life directed, however, lived with purpose that helps heal and rebuild the lives of others has far more meaning than how successful we are. To be aware of who we are, and the abilities we've been given without them being discounted or marginalized by distractions is a life well lived, a life that makes a difference.

Seek not to be the center of attention. Rather, make others the center of yours.

Returning Home

"There's no place like home" means little to those whose memories of early childhood experiences were anything but helpful, but for those who were brought up in families where love and appreciation were considered more important than appearance or performance, the story is different. For them, "home" was a place of acceptance and respect, where opportunities were provided to express and experience themselves in ways that prepared them for years ahead.

Unfortunately, even in the best of families, many of us were taught to live from a place of fear rather than love; to obey, say and do the right things, be good (for goodness sake), for we knew even if our parents were not watching, God was. He was always there, around every corner, making sure we behaved and if we didn't, we knew we'd face consequences far more serious than anything our parents might do.

This way of seeing God as some celestial parole officer out to get us if we misbehaved has, for many, created a God to be feared, a God who requires absolute obedience or else. Is this how it was meant to be, life lived under a cloud, a place of fear, afraid of making a mistake, of not getting it right?

Though we might wish otherwise, our world is built largely on fear; fear of not having enough, fear of failing, of not being accepted, fear of the unknown, of life, of death, of the hereafter, and yes ... fear of the very One who gave us life. Is this what the Creator had in mind when He brought us into the world, that we should constantly be on guard lest we fail or offend him?

No wonder there is this great desire to escape, to find our way home or at least feel at home in a world that is constantly changing, where crime and deception have become the "new normal," where parents feel they must protect their children from forces meant to destroy, and the elderly must be on the lookout for those who would take away what little they have. And to make things even more difficult are the expectations of the One above all others who commands us to obey or face the consequences.

From childhood on, this desire to escape the unrest that surrounds us, to find our way back home, seems to override all other emotions. We may not be able to identify or express these feelings, but they are always there; a sense of being guided by a power greater than ourselves, some mystical force unseen but always present. Perhaps this is why the desire to "return home" to feel secure in a world that is continually changing and experience the Divine anew in ways other than what we've been taught is more than just a preference. It appears to be a driving force behind how we live; the desire to return to a relationship based on love rather than fear.

In one way or another, all of us are trying to find our way out of the world we have created to a place where we can find some meaning beyond the superficial. How to get there when the restraints and restrictions around us are becoming more intense, where confusion seems the norm and much we depended upon has been compromised, is not only challenging but at times overwhelming.

What is it that keeps us trapped in this cycle of frustration and fear that prevents us from experiencing life as it was meant to be? Why is it we feel so out of balance, continually on the move but getting nowhere? Is it possible our desire to escape life as we're experiencing it has more to do with our understanding of God and our relationship to Him than the circumstances that surround us? Could it be God is not "out to get us" but desires to "take us" from a place of fear to an experience of love where His power can transform us into the beings he has always intended us to be?

Though we might wish otherwise, even the best of us can remember times we were definitely not "at our best," times when we said or did things we regret. To recognize experiences where we could have done better is fine, but to allow them to define us and hold us back from who we are now and the possibilities of who we might be tomorrow is not in our best interest or anyone else's for that matter.

Although memories remind us of times we may have acted in ways we are not proud of, we may also remember experiences when the spirit of God entered our lives, powerful enough to awaken us to new levels of consciousness we had not known before. These times of spiritual awakening may have lasted a few moments or longer. The length of time is not as important as the experience itself and what impact these times of awakening have had on our decisions and new directions our lives may have taken.

Remembering those times of spiritual renewal when we felt a special closeness to God rather than the dark places in our journeys is good, but to expect to have the same experiences again in exactly the same way, may not happen, nor should we expect them to.

Like any friendship, we may desire a closer relationship with God but that possibility may not come about if we don't embrace the opportunity we have in this moment and appreciate it for what it is. This feeling of centeredness, a breathing in and breathing out in our relationship to God, might be all that is needed, at least for now. Our times and experiences in meditation might be different too. We must not compare ourselves to others and expect to have a spiritual experience exactly like theirs.

It is true we all come from the same source, but each one of us is unique, special, one of a kind. There are no duplicates. Each snowflake is different. None are identical, nor are we. Our lives are a reflection of what our Creator intended us to be. To admire or even adopt certain methods used by those whose spiritual paths and insights have brought enlightenment to themselves and others is fine, but to try and walk in their footsteps in exactly the same way they have walked may not be possible, nor should it be. We are each different, and our relationship with the One who has given us life is also special and unique.

To walk our own path, rather than become reflections of what we or others expect, ever open to whatever channels of communication connect us to our Creator is enough. For some, a sense of closeness may come through hours spent in meditation. Others find their center through writing, teaching, listening to music, or sitting by a lake reading a book. Still, others find solace and inspiration by climbing a mountain or exploring the unknown on a path they've never been on before, and then there are those who experience a closeness to God while walking along a beach listening to waves pounding the shore - and though forgiveness might be required - yes even while eating an ice cream cone. And if we are present in the moment, even ordinary experiences; washing dishes, talking to a friend, watching lovers holding hands, or a child at play can lift the spirit.

All of life and all relationships in whatever form they are experienced are meant to provide us opportunities to understand and trust the hand that has given us life. This journey we share together was never meant to hurt or destroy but to lift us up to new levels of understanding, an embracing of truths we may not have seen or experienced before.

When we begin to see our Creator as He really is, a God of compassion and love, not a judge ready to condemn but a friend; the barriers that separate us from God and one another will give way to a new experience. Though for each, this spiritual experience may be different, as we continue this adventure we're on and understand more clearly the true nature of divinity; that God's love, the greatest power in the universe, is ever present to see us through whatever we face; fear and anxiety will begin to fade, and we will know we have found our way home not only in this world but ready as well for transition to our new home in the world to come.

*Nature has but one message;
don't try to be what you are not.*

The Best Gifts in Life Are Free

There are thousands, perhaps millions, who long for the gift of eternal life, yet don't know what to do with themselves on a rainy afternoon. To acknowledge one's faith in God and the world to come is fine, but the benefits are few if we are blind to what we have already.

Whether we realize it or not, each day provides us with gifts far more valuable than anything we could ever build or buy. Just waking up in the morning is, in itself, a gift. To share a cup of coffee, a handshake, a hug with a friend or loved one; who could ask for more.

To walk through a field, sit by a stream, or play hide and seek with the shadows as the sun dances across the sky is a present beyond compare. To know the joy of oneness with another, of becoming a parent or a grandparent, is one of the grandest experiences we could ever have.

To know the thrill of climbing a mountain, of experiencing the beauty of a sunrise or sunset with a friend, or just being a kid again in the midst of an old-fashioned rough-and-tumble snowball fight is life at its best.

These are the gifts, the ordinary and the extraordinary, that enrich our lives and prepare us for every tomorrow … and beyond.

Ageless Solutions For A Better Tomorrow

No matter how intricate or grand, nothing is beyond the notice or too small for greatness in the mind of God. Hidden within the tiniest particles of matter are possibilities beyond our ability to see or understand. We are amazed at what God can do with even the smallest of his creations. When given the care required, a tiny seed can become a tree of proportions unimaginable or, when scattered across a field, can feed thousands; a few cells joined together can create the greatest miracle of all, a new addition to life.

We marvel at this mystery of creation, life at its beginnings so small yet with potential that's almost beyond belief. To be part of this process is a miracle in itself, especially when we experience what it's like to become parents, of bringing new life into the world.

At birth, these special family "additions" are completely dependent on those who gave them life and others who care for them. Over time, however, if given the opportunity, they gradually become the unique beings God created them to be, each contributing to life according to the abilities and gifts they've received.

Regardless of who they are or where they were born, all have a purpose in the mind of God. Though we may discount or marginalize them because of their appearance, certain personality traits or unwise choices, the great Creator understands the circumstances of all and sees possibilities in each of his children we may not.

Although we may wish otherwise, we have unfortunately allowed cultural and traditional expectations to restrict and control the creative spirit with which we were born, especially so with the young who are trying to find their way in a world that is extremely confusing and anything but constant.

They continually receive messages through social media from friends and the not-so-friendly who underestimate the potential of the human spirit and remind them of their limitations, that it's safer to stay within the ordinary. They are warned not to attempt too much, to remain near the base of the mountain, that to try and get to the summit is not only dangerous but beyond their ability.

Although our intentions are good, we too are not always as supportive of the young as we could be. We have designed educational systems that require all to meet certain standards with very little regard for personal ability.

To consider each child special with possibilities beyond certain personality traits or appearance takes insight and patience, yet is extremely important if a child is to develop and experience the natural abilities and talents they've inherited. To recognize the potential of each young person and encourage them to become all they were meant to be is the greatest gift we can give them and through them to the world.

By taking into account the character and abilities of each child, we can provide them opportunities to grow and experience life at levels neither we nor they could imagine. The possibilities that lie dormant, undeveloped within each of our children and within each of us, like the potential within a tiny seed, could, if recognized and encouraged, not only make a difference personally but also be a powerful influence of change in the world.

This concept, however, a more personalized approach in educating our young, will not be easy. Even though we see ourselves as a progressive society due to our advanced technology, in other areas, including certain requirements and standards of education, we have a long way to go. Our society has put in place methods and messages through movies and multimedia agencies that are not only confusing to young minds but encourage them to act in ways opposite the ideals and standards by which we say we want them to live. We don't seem to understand much less manage the results of our actions which have caused and continue to create emotional trauma and anger among the young.

Given how far we have come in technology, we often look down on what we consider to be more primitive cultures, yet when examined more closely, many of these so-called uncivilized societies are far in advance of us in addressing the needs of their children. This is especially true in encouraging respect among the young for the elderly and others in positions of authority which in years past was important to us as well but which we seem to have forgotten.

Regardless of ability, they don't idolize the young nor look to them for guidance, but to those of experience who have been around the longest, those of advanced years who are wise and have seen and experienced life in ways of which the young have not yet had the opportunity. They are the ones who are valued, respected, and looked to for guidance. To them, wrinkles are signs of wisdom; old age something to be revered, not slowed down but desired, a place of honor where insight and understanding reside, where experience is not only appreciated but admired.

Unfortunately, like some worn-out appliance or piece of machinery, our culture often marginalizes those of advanced years at the very time when they could contribute the most. Because of certain age limits imposed on them by our society, they are made to feel they can no longer contribute to life as they once did. We have even invented the experience called "retirement," which separates them even further from society. Before it became official, the only retirement people knew was when it was time to leave the planet.

Though we might not fully realize what we have done, in our drive towards a more progressive society, we have marginalized one of the most valuable sources of support the young could have. We've removed the elders, those who have been around the longest and know the most about life, and made them appear obsolete, distancing them from those who could benefit the most from their presence and experience.

Because we have marginalized this important source of support for the young, they turn elsewhere ... to each other, to Hollywood, to music icons not much older than themselves and just as immature, in hopes of finding the support they need or worse yet to chemicals that help them escape the reality of the world we have created.

If we want the new generation and those yet to come to reflect the moral and spiritual standards we expect, then the time has come for us to provide them the resources we can, including and especially a closer relationship between them and those of advanced years, men and women of wisdom and experience. We must rebuild the bridges that have separated the young from the old; bring together those who have been on the journey the longest with those whose journey has just begun.

No, it will not be easy to rebuild relationships that have been neglected or lost, but the benefits to old and young will be worth the effort, and who knows what it might mean to our children and generations to come.

What in the World's Going On?

Though years have gone by, and the old-time carnivals have faded away, who can forget the hall of mirrors we kids of yesteryear enjoyed. Eerie images, spooky and weird, with little bodies and big heads or big bodies with little heads stared back at us and we loved every minute of it.

Like a hall of mirrors, ours is a world of illusions, where truth is often discounted or ignored, replaced by images, reflections of the real. All of us are affected by this "Alice in Wonderland" syndrome whether we realize it or not. Through entertainment and advertising, multimedia experts allure millions into accepting the superficial as norm and appearances as real.

Across the centuries, great minds from almost every tradition have affirmed the truth of the oneness of the human family, yet we still imagine ourselves to be separate from one another and have demonstrated this illusion by creating a world more fragmented than ever. We are no closer to healthy relationships now than when warriors from the past showed their military might by throwing stones at each other. The only change is the size of our stones. We still can't get along. Separatism has become our mantra, and unity an illusion.

What is it about our lifestyles that cause us to ignore the obvious and accept the imaginary? Who cast the spell that has imprisoned us in a land of make-believe? What in the world's going on?

Perhaps it's time we took a closer look at the truth behind our illusions, re-examined the distorted images we've put in place, the processes and thinking that deepen the rifts between us, that give mixed messages and continue to move us and our children in directions that are unacceptable and jeopardize our future.

It's obvious we've made progress in science and technology, but our advance as a human race is questionable. Ways of thinking that put in place inconsistent and convoluted systems within our lives and communities, that limit expression and opportunity, giving advantage to some while withholding it from others, is not a sign of progress.

To hold on to systems of belief - social, political, or religious - that promote an "ours is the only way" mind-set, disregarding or disrespecting the traditions and cultural values of others, that deepen a sense of isolation and separation, is not progressive.

To stand behind facades, under the guise of confidentiality as individuals, organizations, or as a nation, intentionally withholding, or giving incomplete or inaccurate information to those dependent upon it in making important decisions, is not a sign of progress.

To seek profit through questionable policies or business practices that take advantage of those with limited resources, jeopardizing their ability to meet daily commitments and undermining their future security is not progressive (nor "profitable").

To be sensitive, even indignant at the inhumane treatment of some animals, while ignoring billions of others simply because they are food on our tables, is not a sign of progress.

To undermine the delicate balance of nature, exploiting earth's limited resources, bringing comfort and opportunity to some while the majority have little or nothing, is not progressive.

To enrich entertainers or sports heroes at the expense of those who seek to strengthen the values society is based upon is not a sign of progress.

Few would challenge our standing among nations as a superpower. We are the richest, most powerful nation on earth, yet the poor and homeless continue to suffer, and we seem incapable or unwilling to do anything about it. As a nation, our contributions to the less fortunate nationally and worldwide are significant. Compared to our resources, however, we give little of what we could to relieve the desperation and poverty around us. Caught up in the bigger, better, more syndrome, greed has superseded generosity, and getting and saving have become the measure of success rather than giving and sharing,

We spend millions – make that billions - on diets, health food fads, and on research to "find a cure," and have a health care system second to none, yet our health issues are among the most critical on the planet, and we die of diseases almost unheard of in less affluent parts of the world.

We have strict standards set by regulatory organizations that prohibit the use of unapproved drugs. If, however, the drugs are popular and financially viable, such as alcohol and tobacco, their use, with some restrictions, is generally accepted and often encouraged in spite of the thousands of lives lost each year, children neglected and abused, or families destroyed.

We are a nation that prides itself on records and have now moved into first place ahead of China and Russia with a new record. We now have the most citizens imprisoned of any country in the world. Given the apparent ineffectiveness of our rehabilitation programs, we are continuing our emphasis on control and containment by expanding our judicial services and constructing more detention centers.

We are extremely concerned about our children and their future, yet we allow them to sit in front of computers, TV screens, watch movies and provide other forms of entertainment that expose them to influences and behaviors opposite our values, then wring our hands and shake our heads in disbelief when violence erupts in our schools and communities and the more vulnerable act out what they have learned.

We are concerned about global warming and yet, according to reliable sources, there are technologies available today and have been for decades (many illegally classified) that could completely transform our dependence on fossil fuels. Were it not for special interest groups, their military and economic agendas, and the conflicts that result from both, these advanced technologies could have been on the market years ago, providing us and our world with energy systems more efficient and less contaminating than anything presently available.

We are strong in our support of human rights and hold other nations accountable when those rights are abused. If asked, however, to help end the misery of someone whose condition has become unbearable through disease and suffering, we are told it's against the law. It's called a "criminal offense." If, on the other hand, it meets our political or economic agendas (or policies of "non-interference in internal affairs"), the taking or allowing of thousands of lives to be taken against their will through judicial or military action, even if it means some unfortunate "collateral damage" is not only permitted but encouraged. We call it "protecting our freedoms."

We use force to control force, violence to fight violence, and terror against terrorists and seem surprised that our methods fuel discontent and madness instead of the peace and calm we seek. In the midst of the chaos and noise of battle, we honor our fallen heroes while the "enemy" honors theirs. Dreams of a better world have fallen prey to our inconsistencies and illusions.

Our religious traditions hold places of honor in our hearts and in our society, and so they should. When "truth," however, becomes disconnected, an end in itself and takes on an aura of superiority, disregarding the rights and liberties of others, some of the most hideous crimes against humanity, as history has proven, have been instigated and carried out by religious organizations. Even today, much of the strife we see in war-torn countries of the world is religiously motivated.

Concerns for our children, our children's children and future generations are more apparent and more urgent now than ever before, however these concerns are being undermined by patterns of behavior that continue to move us in directions that compromise their future. Many of our financial institutions have collapsed and though our economy at home and abroad may seem to be getting stronger, as a nation we are trillions in debt.

Standards of education that have for years made us leaders internationally are declining, and given the recent crisis of fear generated and fueled by the media that has compromised the lives and livelihoods of millions, and has caused the closure of thousands of our colleges, universities and elementary schools, our children's future and their dreams have been further compromised.

Our health care system is becoming more difficult to maintain financially, with millions unable to afford even the basics of health care coverage. The inequities between the "haves" and "have not's" are becoming greater. Third-world countries are doing more with less, while more advanced countries are doing less with more. The effects of global warming are no longer the territory of misguided minds but a reality. Greed, power, and control have taken over the lives of much of our leadership at the expense of those they were meant to serve. Terrorism, internal, external, and imagined, is taking away our freedoms. Intolerance of others' views and ways of life, cultures, and traditions is no longer the exception but the norm. The mechanisms of war are becoming more sophisticated, and international conflicts more common.

The unrest and strife around us are not the results of some preordained or predetermined outcome but of the illusion we have embraced and lived out … the imagined idea that we are separate from one another, separate from our environment and from the very source of life itself. Over the centuries and millennia this illusion of separation has become so dominant in human thinking that thoughts to the contrary appear abnormal.

To think we can have the advantage of an abundant life and optimum health, while others know nothing but illness and premature death is an illusion. To suggest we can succeed while others have little choice beyond failure is an illusion. To assume we can be safe and secure in our nation or community while others are constantly at risk is an illusion. To believe ourselves to be free when others are abused and enslaved is an illusion. To seek peace in our corner of the world when the world at large is in turmoil and conflict is an illusion. To think we are separate from anything or anyone and can act irresponsibly or disregard the needs of others outside our cultural circles without it impacting our lives is an illusion.

Lost in a world of shadows and make-believe, we seem oblivious to the signs that point us toward peace and keep throwing over barrier after barrier meant to protect us. Slowly, systematically we are destroying the very support system that makes life on earth sustainable. As if mesmerized by some sinister force, we continue dream-like on a journey to nowhere, moving ever closer to the edge of existence.

Visionaries from ancient times and indigenous peoples from traditions and cultures all over the world, many of whom are outside traditional circles, warn of coming events brought about by greed, power, and control, an obsession with the material that disrespects human life, and disregards the environment that could be cataclysmic in nature, of a magnitude beyond our ability to anticipate much less prepare for. Soon so they say, mother nature will discipline her unruly children.

Our civilization has now reached a crossroads. Wonderful possibilities and opportunities lie ahead for us and our children if we make the right decisions, but if we continue moving in the direction we are now, life on planet earth will soon become unsustainable.

Dreams of a better world are not enough. Now is the time to re-examine the traditions, political ideologies, religious persuasions, and racial prejudices that separate us. Now is the time to replace our cultural and traditional differences with an appreciation for the richness of diversity, removing those barriers that separate, tearing down walls that suppress and isolate.

Now is the time to put our energies and resources into creating peace in place of war, uplifting rather than tearing down, sharing instead of hoarding, contributing to life rather than exploiting it, cooperating rather than competing, giving the advantage rather than taking it, serving instead of subduing. Now is the time to experience and express higher levels of consciousness, a deeper understanding of life, and a renewed sense of the interconnectedness of all living things.

Now is the time to give expression to the overwhelming desire of the human heart to know and experience unity and peace. Now is the time to move beyond the boundaries that separate us into a new experience, a new age, a new world; a world of compassion and understanding; a world that respects the rights of all peoples and gives equal opportunities to all … "One World, under God, indivisible, with liberty and justice for all."

- *When we are born, we cry and the world is happy; when we die the world cries, and we are happy.*

- *Communication respects differences, strengthens relationships, and creates opportunity … not negotiations.*

Special Section

The following essays address those holidays which are celebrated or at least recognized by a majority in the Western World – such as Christmas and the New Year. Also included in this section is an essay entitled "A Cry of Innocence," a closer look at the Newtown, Connecticut, tragedy, lessons learned, and those yet to be learned.

Christmas – A Time to Remember

Soon another year will fade into memory, but before we say goodbye to the old and bring in the new, there's one last tradition that families and communities across our nation will celebrate before the new year begins. Through pageantry, poetry, and song and in ways shaped by centuries of celebration, Christmas will once again enter our lives.

Although short, this special time of year allows us a brief respite from our professions, our responsibilities, our cares, and our concerns. Suddenly we're transported into a landscape overflowing with sights and sounds almost beyond magical. We're children again, dancing, playing, singing, and laughing, carefree and alive.

Christmas is a time when the ordinary becomes extraordinary. It's a time for giving and receiving, a time to forget and a time to remember, a time for playfulness and sharing, a time to allow our senses and imaginations to embrace the wonder and beauty of what is truly an enchanting, magical time of year.

Above all, it provides us the opportunity of breaking away from the intensity of our lives, away from the superficial and artificial. It gives us a chance to remember and renew those relationships that have enriched and brought meaning to our lives. It reminds us, too, that no matter our cultural or ethnic backgrounds, we share a common heritage. We are all members of the same family.

As we reach out with compassion and understanding throughout this season and the new year ahead, removing whatever separates us from one another, respecting and appreciating each other's similarities as well as differences, we become instruments of change, a unifying presence in our communities and in our world ... a reflection of what the true spirit of this season is all about.

Holiday Memories

Although time has moved on far more quickly than I could have imagined, childhood memories of days gone by still remain, especially those magical moments called holidays.

Who could forget the aroma of mashed potatoes and gravy, turkey, cranberry sauce, and pumpkin pie for dessert? Our table was set for a king, and even though we were far from well-to-do, ours was a feast indeed, leaving no doubt about our royal heritage, especially at Thanksgiving. Like others, our family wasn't perfect, but as we gathered around this table of plenty, expressing our gratitude for the simple, ordinary gifts of life, there was a deepening of appreciation for each other and for those experiences shared in common that brought us together and kept us together as a family.

As Thanksgiving with turkey and all the trimmings faded away, our community evolved into a magical land of make-believe. Houses, once dark and uninviting, were now places of interest, destinations for sight-seers. There were reindeer and sleighs, elves and singing minstrels, candles, wreathes, and colored lights designed to hold the attention of young and old alike. This was the Disneyland that I knew long before there was a destination by that name. Yes, Christmas had come again, and my childhood heart was filled with wonder at the beauty and magic of it all.

Towards the beginning of December, my parents, sister, and I checked out the evergreens at a Christmas tree lot not far from our home. Even though prices had gone through the roof (75 cents), we went ahead, paid the attendant, tied the tree securely to the roof of our car, and headed home. Once inside, the aroma of evergreen filled the house, and before long, with the help of mom, dad, and some little hands, our tree became anything but ordinary. It was absolutely beautiful, a work of art covered in tinsel and crowned with an angel.

As Christmas Eve drew near and presents under the tree grew as well, so did the excitement of two little people, especially me. I was the youngest in the family, and even though I was very shy, I managed to get up enough courage to sit on Santa's knee at one of the big department stores in town and tell him what I wanted for Christmas. Of course, there was no doubt in my little mind that he would deliver just as he promised.

Like other children, I too had been told of Santa's amazing journey around the world, bringing candy canes, toys, and special presents to "good boys and girls." And since I had been a good boy, well at least most the time, certainly Santa wouldn't forget me! Right?

And indeed he didn't, even though his arrival wasn't exactly the way I had expected. You see, our family lived in the South and there was no snow or at least very little. That's probably why I didn't see any reindeer or sleigh.

I did hear him, though, late at night on Christmas Eve. Though he didn't come down our chimney, his arrival was just as exciting. With my heart in my throat and eyes as big as saucers, I listened to the sound of heavy boots coming up our basement steps. Suddenly with a "HO, HO, HO," our basement door opened, and there he was, the man in red with the white flowing beard. And me, I was frozen in place, unable to move. It was fantastic, unbelievable, but true! Santa had come! I was not forgotten!

Memories. How special. As my mind wanders back across the years to that time when childhood dreams and fantasies came true, I find myself wishing that I could go back to those good ole days, that I could be a child again, exploring once more that place of innocence where imagination and reality were one and the same.

Is it possible? Can we go back? Could we become children again?

We may not be able to erase the years, but the child within is still there and, when given the chance, is ready to make every holiday a celebration and each day a grand adventure.

> *The heart always knows what is true even if the mind disagrees.*

The Spirit of the Season

Though family traditions and customs may differ, Christmas is still observed by many as a time for remembering those special moments and people who mean so much to us. It's a celebration that had its beginnings in the past yet shapes the present. Over the centuries it has established itself deep within the psyche of our western world. Through pageantry, poetry and song, we are reminded once again of a humble birth and an extraordinary life that has influenced the course of nations for centuries.

As with Christmases past, this time of year gives us an opportunity to back away from the routine, from our professions, our responsibilities, our cares and concerns, and know again the love and warmth of family and friends. Though brief, in a sense, Christmas transcends time. We enter a landscape overflowing with sights and sounds, both mysterious and magical. For a little while we can move back to childhood again, dancing, playing, singing, and laughing, carefree and alive.

Although this is the experience shared by many, unfortunately for others the story is different. For those who wrestle with addictions, chronic illnesses, separation, divorce, memories of friends or relatives who have passed away, or whose lives have been touched by loss in other ways, the holidays can be very difficult.

To be more sensitive to those whose loneliness and suffering are intensified during the holidays is just as much "in the spirit of the season" as anything else we might celebrate or be involved in.

To share a smile, a handshake, a tear, a hug; to reach out in love and understanding to those who know nothing but sadness and despair, who feel depressed, abandoned, lost, is to bring a new dimension of meaning to the holiday season.

By bringing hope and healing to those in need, we enrich their lives as well as our own. If allowed, the gift of love – the spirit of giving – could very well turn holidays into "holy days."

What we give to others can never be taken away.

Christmas – A Time for Embracing The "Present"

Christmas has a beauty and uniqueness few other holidays have. It's a time of celebration, of remembering, of renewing relationships. Though brief, it provides a window of opportunity through which we can escape reality and become children again.

Enchanted by a thousand lights, colorful storefronts, and a hundred Santas, it's easy, however, to get lost in a fantasyland of make-believe. Beyond the brightly decorated gifts reserved for loved ones is another gift more important than all the rest. It is the spirit of compassion and love, reaching out to the discouraged, the sick, or the unfortunate.

For many, the holidays are a reminder of Christmases past, of memories tucked away in the corridors of time, of loved ones, friends, and family who are no longer around. It's a time when we are once again reminded of the mystery and wonder of life and the importance of those whose love and presence enrich our lives. To celebrate the present and embrace the moment and those relationships that bring meaning to our lives is one of the greatest presents of all, for no matter how grand the gift, it means nothing if there's no one there to receive it. To give a hug, hold a hand, and be there for those we care about, realizing that next Christmas they might not be around, makes all other gifts fade in comparison.

Regardless of circumstances, the "present" – the here and now – is a gift we can all share. To do so could make this holiday season one of the brightest and grandest ever.

> ✽ *When love is present, nothing else is needed, nor does anything else matter.*

To Broadway With Love

Although doubtful it will ever hit Broadway, much less Hollywood, there's a new play in the works. The actors may not be professional, but they certainly have potential. The parts they decide on and whether the play will be a success or not is yet to be determined. Even though the script is not complete, the play will begin on time as it always has.

Like all before, this production is a mixture of drama, comedy, high adventure, and more than enough suspense. Acting ability is not limited to the most talented but to all, regardless of background or experience. Actors are not chosen but choose whatever character or part they wish to play.

Now that the stage is set and the choreography underway, stagehands, technical support, and actors are getting ready for a series of rehearsals that could lead to one of the most important productions in recent years.

Performers of all ages are allowed, encouraged actually, to take on personalities and characters they feel most comfortable with. Choices are broad and range from the elite and powerful to the ordinary and poor, from the courageous and skilled to the fearful and inexperienced.

Authenticity requires each actor to thoroughly immerse themselves in the disposition, thoughts, and feelings of the particular role or character they choose. Though subtle, actors are often drawn towards roles with which they are familiar or embody similarities to their own way of thinking or living. Some take on personalities that are more self-centered, controlling, and insensitive, while others move towards roles where compassion, kindness, and understanding are of more importance. Some choose to be in the center of things, the spotlight, and applause, while others feel more comfortable in supportive roles.

Soon dress rehearsals will be completed, and the production itself will be on stage. Although the play, scheduled to run from January 1 to December 31 of the New Year, will not remain on Broadway as long as most productions, it should be long enough to know how well the actors work together and what kind of impact they have on their audiences. Hopefully, this play will be a great success, far beyond any that have preceded it, but that's up to the actors. Guess we'll just have to wait and see as the curtain rises on a new year.

A New Beginning

Another year will soon begin, another opportunity to tell the story of life on planet earth. The unknown is just ahead, a new adventure into the unexplored and unexpected. The terrain may be unfamiliar and conditions far from ideal, but retreating to the comfortable and familiar is not an option.

As with years past, this year too is wrapped in mystery. What it will bring will largely be determined by our choices rather than something preordained or predestined. Some have suggested this might be a year of transition, of dramatic change for the human race, a time of trouble as some philosophers and theologians predict.

Visionaries from ancient times and indigenous peoples from traditions and cultures around the world share a similar view, warning of events just ahead that could be of a magnitude beyond our ability to anticipate, much less prepare for.

Regardless of what lies ahead, our world has definitely reached a crossroads in the way we live and relate to each other. Depending on the decisions we make, wonderful opportunities for us and our children are within our reach, but if we continue moving in the direction we are now, life as we know it on planet earth will be unsustainable.

Throughout the year ahead, we will once again be given the opportunity to tear down the boundaries that separate us, transform the world we have created into a world that respects everyone's rights regardless of race or background.

This is the world our children and our children's children deserve. Are we willing to honor and appreciate our differences and provide them with a better future? The days ahead are unknown, but they may have more to do with who we are and the decisions we make than we realize. We can make a difference ... if we so choose. Life is truly an **a-maz-ing** experience.

> 🕊 *Life is like a maze. There are stops, starts, beginnings, and endings, but if we keep going, eventually we will find the way. Life truly is an **a-maz-ing** experience.*

A Cry of Innocence

Newtown, Connecticut – Sandy Hook Elementary School

What do you say to six-year-olds in shock, terrified, who just ran from their school to your house, from something so unthinkable, so unbelievable, the mind can't take it in?

"We can't go back to school. We can't. We have no teacher. Our teacher is dead!"

How do you explain to children just beginning to live that something unimaginable has just taken their friends, their playmates, and their teachers away, never to return? How do you comfort a parent who just lost a child or heal a community that just lost twenty of their children and six of their finest teachers? And what do you say to a nation that feels the pain of this once peaceful community?

How could something so unexpected, so tragic, happen in a place of innocence and learning, a place surrounded by woods and beautiful homes? Could the taking of innocent lives have been prevented? The answers, if there are any, won't come easy.

In light of the Newtown tragedy, many have called for tighter restrictions on gun control, the arming of private citizens, a greater police presence, and safer protocols for our schools. Others have suggested more funding in support of treatment programs for those with mental health issues.

Few would disagree these concerns need to be addressed, but is this enough?

As a society, our way of dealing with violence is to put in place measures that either control or modify human behavior. Although methods may differ, over the centuries indigenous peoples and advanced cultures around the world have used this approach, but the results have been less than encouraging. To expect radical change through external means of control without addressing deeper issues will, as history has proven, be limited at best. Although worn by overuse, the definition of insanity – doing the same old thing in the same old way, expecting different results – might not be too far from the truth.

Though unintentional, could it be our lifestyles have created an environment where deviant behavior is not only allowed but encouraged, where loss of life caused by those with mental or emotional disorders or overwhelming stress has become too common?

Perhaps we need to look more closely at the reasons behind destructive behaviors that weaken our society; reexamine messages given our young that undermine principles of honesty and integrity.

To teach our children that character and integrity are more important than outward appearance, that true worth from within is of more value than fame or fortune, and then expose them to images and messages on DVDs and computers, in theaters, and at checkout counters that teach them the opposite, does not work.

To educate our young in technology and the arts and sciences but fail to guide them in the basics of human behavior and healthy relationships does not work.

To use the same energy that caused a problem to prevent it by arming a nation so the good can protect themselves against the not-so-good, does not work.

As a human family, somehow we must find a way to go deeper in dealing with patterns of thinking and behavior that continue to undermine the life we say we want for ourselves and our children. To continue to give double messages to young people and expect them, especially those at higher risk, to somehow become balanced, compassionate human beings is a type of logic that leaves much to be desired. It stretches the imagination beyond reasonable limits.

Whether individuals, communities, or as a nation, unless and until human behavior is closely examined by addressing cause and effect issues, progress will be an illusion and terror will once again rise to haunt us.

It's time to face the truth. The old ways of transforming society through external restrictions and force are not working. They are temporary at best. If we want to see a better world for ourselves and our children, we must choose again. We cannot continue along the course we're on now.

A new approach that addresses change from within, that encourages respect for the rights of all and sees everyone regardless of color, gender, education, or religion, as legitimate, deserving members of the human family – our family – is what is needed if we ever hope to stop the violence that has taken over our nation and our world. This new approach may not bring about immediate results, but in time it could make ... all the difference in the world.

We can learn from the past, but we can't live there. When we let go of the past, the past will let go of us.

Reflections

- When we see things as they really are, we will know everything is meant to bring us exactly what we need.
- Our worth has nothing to do with what we have and everything to do with who we are.
- Tributes to the mind last for decades; monuments in stone last for centuries, but that which honors the heart and spirit lasts forever.
- It's the struggles, the reaching out beyond ourselves, that makes us who we are.
- Life must be seen through the prism of love, otherwise nothing makes sense.
- Permanence is an illusion; change is forever.
- Life is a journey of choice, not chance.
- Life comes with no guarantees, just opportunity.
- It's the ordinary things that make life extraordinary.
- To profit at the expense of others is a very poor investment.
- Spend your life; that's what it's for.

- Only when we accept and love ourselves unconditionally, can we love and accept others unconditionally.
- Healing takes place within ourselves when we reach out to help others
- A life lived to bless is far greater than a life lived to impress.
- Pleasure is external; joy is eternal. One is temporary; the other forever.
- It's not the place but the experience that matters.
- How well off we are is not as important as how well off we leave others.
- Clarity comes through the heart, not the mind.
- Those who have been through the most are often the ones who give the most.
- When our journey on earth comes to an end, we will be remembered more for who we have been than for what we have done.
- The mind is blind; only the heart can see.

- What we see in ourselves, we become; what we see in others, they become.
- To be who you are and where you are is enough. Nothing else is expected or needed.
- There is no greater gift than the "present."
- Where there's a choice, health is far better than wealth.
- If you want to see the Divine, look in the mirror and into the faces of all whose paths cross your own.
- Dogs bark behind chain-linked fences to protect that which is not their own. Humans often do the same.
- We often see our defects and overlook our strengths. If, however, we see our strengths and overlook our defects, chances are good, others will do the same.
- Because our perceptions are so limited, it might be in our best interest at times to allow things to fall apart.
- Mirrors tell us what we look like but not who we are.
- Some of the most attractive people often come in forms that leave much to be desired.
- Love enables; fear disables.

- It is often better to want what you have than to have what you want.
- Obsessions and addictions are often the results when the natural need for love and acceptance is denied.
- Our virtues and our vices might be more closely related than we think.
- Embrace life, and life will embrace you.
- Unconditional love requires nothing.
- Our religions limit or strengthen our understanding of the Divine, both of which determine how we live.
- Nature has but one message; don't try to be what you are not.
- Outside of time, age does not exist.
- Unity comes about through cooperation, not competition.
- God dwells in heaven. Where God is not cannot be.
- What matters is not how much time we spend but who we spend it with, not where we go, but who goes with us.

- To be a light is far better than having our name in lights.
- We are destined to be whatever we choose to be.
- Religion is selective; spirituality embraces all.
- The purpose of life is to live a life that matters, not accumulate matter.
- Bless others with your presence (presents).
- When the natural is treated as unnatural, unnatural things result; when the unnatural is treated as natural, the results are also unnatural.
- When the mouth is closed, people think you are wise. When it is open, they know otherwise.
- We will live very small lives if who we are is determined by the approval or disapproval of others.
- Pleasure is external; joy is eternal.
- Who we are informs, deforms, or transforms what we do.
- Addictions are distractions that divert us from our greatest potential.

- The door to wisdom opens when the mind is quiet, the body still, and the soul is allowed to speak.
- When we appreciate what we have, we will always have enough.
- Generosity creates abundance; greed takes it away.
- There is never enough of what you don't need.
- When we live to give, loss is merely imagined; when we live to get, gain is imagined, and loss is a reality.
- The only way out is within.
- Whether products or pleasure, most advertising changes "desire" to "need" and promotes the results as "happiness."
- The more policies and laws required, the more primitive the society.
- The Divine speaks to our hearts through the world of nature but cannot be heard until the world we have created is silenced.
- Could it be that heaven has more to do with a relationship than a destination?

- The mind tells us what is logical; intuition what is true.
- Since in reality we own nothing; when something is taken away, nothing is lost.
- No matter the form, all creation is an expression of the Divine.
- Life must be lived inside out otherwise everything looks upside down.
- What we give to others can never be taken away.
- Unconditional love never forces and has no requirements.
- To stop judging others, we must stop judging ourselves.
- The Creator has made provision for every natural desire to be expressed and experienced.
- Don't put people in their place; help them find their place.
- Change is not possible until the religion of the mind becomes a relationship of the heart.
- Each moment provides opportunities for new beginnings.

- We must remember where we came from to know where we are going.
- Success is defined by how much we love, not how much we know.
- Death is temporary. Transition and change are forever.
- A religion of the mind needs requirements; that of the spirit needs nothing.
- More often than not the mind has a mind of its own. It distracts us from living in the present ... whenever it has a mind to.
- Life has nothing to do with what we hold in our hands, only what we hold in our hearts.
- No matter how attractive, an instrument only has value when it is played.
- When we reach out with love and compassion to meet the needs of others, our own needs will be met.
- At times we miss seeing the beauty around us because we're looking in the wrong direction.
- It's only when we embrace the darkness that we can appreciate the light.

- Life seldom comes to us as we desire or expect. It comes in ways often unexpected or unacceptable but when allowed has power to transform.
- The present is all there is. We cannot see a sunrise, feel the rain dance on our faces, or appreciate the beauty of a flower yesterday or tomorrow - only in the moment. There is No Other Way.
- God never interferes with our choices but is always present to encourage us to make the best choices.
- When we go within, we will never go without.
- It's a law of the universe. We can only keep that which we give away.
- What we do is temporary; who we are is eternal.
- Don't let the past condemn or the future control. Embrace the moment, for only in the present can life be lived, and change be experienced.
- Sometimes we need to be removed from the center of things so we can become more centered.
- Life is a journey of the heart, not the mind.

- God never lets us down, only lifts us up.
- The Divine never directs and then neglects.
- Life is like a maze. There are stops, starts, beginnings, and endings, but if we keep going, eventually we will find our way. Life is truly an *a – maz – ing* experience.
- It is a law of the universe that the more we possess, the less we have, and the more we give, the richer we become.
- Satisfaction from abstinence is far better than pleasure from indulgence.
- The best way to enter a person's life is through their heart.
- The past only has value if it makes us more loving and compassionate today.
- The greatest gift we can give others is to encourage them to be themselves.
- Strength comes through exercise, not observation.
- Our acceptance of others depends largely on our acceptance of ourselves.

- Our worth comes not from whom we know or what we've done, but from who we are.
- The tighter we hold on to what we possess, the less we have and the smaller we become.
- We cannot help someone we don't love or someone we judge.
- How we relate to others is more a reflection of who we are than who they are.
- To be silent is better than to speak and say nothing.
- There's nothing too small for God to notice and nothing too big for God to handle.
- A life centered on others is magnificent; a life centered on self is insignificant.
- Be careful lest illusions become your reality and reality becomes your illusion.
- No matter how dense the darkness, only the light should determine how we live.
- It's vision that holds us back, not resources.
- Neither success nor failure is dependent upon or defined by the praise or disapproval of others.

- Change created by outside requirement is temporary; change from within is permanent.
- To live life the way it was meant to be lived, we must see beyond the seen, touch the untouchable, hear that which is beyond hearing, and embrace a reality beyond our own.
- Is it possible in our intense desire to understand Divine revelations of the past, we become unable or unaware of God revealing Himself in the present?
- In the world of nature, everything is perfect just the way it is. Nothing has to be proven.
- That which lives unto itself will eventually cease to exist.
- Happiness comes from accepting whatever comes our way, not everything going our way.
- Great power in the hands of small minds is destructive.
- Don't tell others where to go. Lead them.
- When we are born, we cry, and the world is happy; when we die, the world cries, and we are happy.
- People and nations change by choice, not by force.

- Love allows.
- We must not be quick to judge that which we do not understand or condemn that which is unfamiliar.
- God often wakes us up to give us rest.
- Caring creates communication.
- What we are attracted to empowers or weakens.
- Love sees the best in the worst and perfection in that which appears imperfect.
- When the heart desires to bless, all the resources needed to bring this about will be provided.
- Tis human to become who we are not; divine to become who we are.
- Happiness is a choice, not an experience.
- If you think everyone will accept and praise you, that nothing you do or say will offend … then you have either been translated or you're living on another planet.
- To acquire what you want at the expense of what you need is a very poor investment.

- Never condemn what the Divine provides, even if tradition and culture disagree.
- What matters is not what you have but who you are.
- God relates to all his creation through commitment, not commandment.
- Everything external will fall into place when everything internal is put in place.
- If we become servants to that which we have created, the end of life as we know it will become a reality.
- Love respects the beliefs and traditions of others. It allows them freedom to become whatever they choose.
- When the heart speaks, words are not necessary.
- Truth is not something to be found; it is something to be experienced.
- Our understanding of God is infinitely small, and our understanding of each other is about the same.
- Time slows down when we do.
- We can learn from the past, but we can't live there. When we let go of the past, the past will let go of us.

- Who we are can only be measured from the inside out, not outside in.
- God speaks to us in a thousand different ways, and always with the same message. "I will do you no harm. The harm is not knowing this."
- God is only limited in that he can only reveal himself to us along those paths with which we are familiar and only by how open we are to receive.
- Passion regards form and disregards spirit. Love respects both.
- Seek not to be the center of attention. Rather, make others the center of yours.
- Don't let your mind run away with your intelligence.
- The mind can lead you astray; intuition shows you the way.
- We play our games as if they were real and treat the real as if they were games.
- Our work is not to convince others to accept our understanding of truth but to open them to their own.
- Don't try to control time. It can take care of itself.

- Surrender to the moment. If you've forgotten how, nature will teach you.
- When you know intuitively what is best, don't worry about what other people think ... most the time, they don't.
- God never inspires us to move forward to become less.
- There is nothing in life that limits us except ourselves.
- To truly love others without conditions is to touch the heart of God.
- Though outside the accepted norms of the day, do not judge what God provides or the way in which it is provided.
- Greed is never satisfied, nor is generosity ever exhausted.
- Allowing the body to express itself in ways with which the heart and soul disagree undermines respect for others and compromises who we are.
- Sometimes we must step back in order to move forward, slow down in order to catch up, stand still in order to make progress.

- Ego says our value comes from what we possess. Spirit says our value comes from what possesses us. Ego says you are what you have. Spirit says ... you are and that's enough.
- Give others the advantage, don't take it.
- You may not be able to prevent a person from falling, but you can help them up.
- Our society tells us we must earn our keep and keep what we earn. Neither is correct.
- The hand that creates always provides.
- Do not be concerned about how you sound or whom you impress. Be concerned instead for where you are bound and whom you can bless.
- Unconditional love has no requirements or expectations. If it does, it is not unconditional.
- As a lake reflects the beauty of that which surrounds it, so too will our lives reflect that by which we choose to be surrounded.
- Through daily communion with the Divine, we will come to understand the reason for our existence. Ways

and means will open before us that will make the impossible possible and the ordinary extraordinary.

- The only way to open the heart is to still the mind.
- We cannot appreciate the light if we know nothing of darkness.
- We pay dearly when our choices and decisions are made from a place of fear.
- We don't need to know it all; we only need to know the One who does.
- God never shuts doors that are meant to be opened.
- Let me surround you with all that I am, so you might become all that you are.
- Power is external. It has to prove itself. Strength comes from within. It need prove nothing yet influences everything.
- That which lives unto itself cannot survive.
- Happiness heals.
- Relationships are strengthened not by what we look at but by what we overlook.

- People may forget what we've done, but they will never forget who we are.
- The more we have, the more time it takes to care for it all, and the less time there is to enjoy the simple and more important things in life.
- The mind analyzes. The heart responds.
- Give everything, require nothing, and you will never be disappointed.
- All temptations are the same, illusions the Creator is withholding something in our best interest.
- There is little cost to exercise, but the price is extremely high without it.
- Our definition of pleasure defines who we are.
- Distractions take us away from the present along paths that go nowhere.
- To be well off is not the same as better off.
- Those who volunteer to correct the faults of others are often the ones in greatest need themselves.
- Walls meant to protect can also isolate.

- Freedom is the caldron by which the soul evolves and creates itself anew.
- Nothing in our best interest and consistent with love is ever kept from us.
- We must take time to rest if we expect to be fully awake.
- Don't let your mind stand in the way of the desires of your heart.
- The choices we make either limit or create opportunities.
- People who know it all seldom contribute much at all.
- Whether theologies, sacred traditions, or cultural values, whatever separates us from one another, is out of harmony with the spirit and power of love upon which all creation is based.
- God cannot speak to us if we've already made up our minds about who he is.
- To try and live in the past or future is to exist in a land of make-believe.

- In the divine scheme of things, nothing is withheld from us that is consistent with love.
- Healing takes place from the inside out, not the outside in.
- Just "be," and I will do the "rest."
- Love honors and respects every … body.
- Live fearlessly. Love fully.
- Care and compassion measure progress, not technology
- Treat every - body, including your own, with respect.
- The physical may bring us together, but only love can keep us together.
- To bring pleasure to the body at the cost of the soul is extremely expensive.
- Among the poorest people in the world are those who have the most but give the least.
- Open my eyes that I may see; Open my heart that I may receive.
- It's the struggles, the reaching out beyond ourselves that move us to new heights and new experiences.

- Could it be what we don't see is real and what we think we see is not?
- Love is the definition of the Divine, not a characteristic.
- Communication respects differences strengthens relationships and creates opportunity, not negotiations.
- When the heart is silenced, and the mind takes control, the results are never in our best interest.
- Sometimes we must become less so we can become more.
- Life is a process of discovering who we are.
- The Divine often comes to us through channels with which we are unfamiliar.
- Be gentle with your body. In fact, be gentle with everybody.
- Ownership is an illusion and, if taken seriously, can be fatal.
- As in ages of old, people do what they are told.
- The results are not in our best interest if the mind is allowed to rule and intuition and insight are marginalized.

- In ultimate reality, there are no endings, only beginnings.
- Whether for gain or pleasure, love never takes advantage of another.
- Passion sees form and disregards the person within. Love sees and honors the person within, regardless of form.
- A response from the heart always takes priority over a response from the mind.
- It's not the place but the experience that makes the difference.
- Ignorance may be bliss, but it can also disrupt or destroy.
- Success is a statement of who we are, not what we do.
- Our lives are perfectly imperfect and perfectly suited to each person's life experience.
- A life lived solely through the body and the mind is transitory but when expressed through the soul is eternal.

- Out of the silence life begins anew; out of the darkness the dawn of a new day begins.
- We will eventually leave the planet, but not life.
- When we enter the silence, we move into a reality that is timeless and eternal.
- Surround yourself with love and your life will be transformed. Surround yourself with fear and that will be your experience.
- All that is seen was created by the unseen, the creative power that brought all that is into existence.
- Passion uncontrolled takes that which is beautiful and destroys it whereas love sees beauty everywhere and creates more of the same.
- Use your time wisely; otherwise it will be a very poor investment.
- No matter the circumstances, when time is taken for communion with the Divine, peace and rest will be ours regardless of what's happening around us.

- All relationships that experience a sense of oneness on the physical level are but reflections of the connection experienced spiritually.
- Love energizes; fear immobilizes.
- We cannot change others, but as our lives are transformed, others are encouraged to change as well.
- Life, as understood by all species, is meant to be celebrated.
- Respect for our similarities as well as our differences will benefit us far more than trying to destroy that which does not fit into our cultural or religious beliefs.
- To embrace life fully, physical intimacy is not required … only love.
- Providing help when not requested may do more harm than good.
- Though the Divine has no form with which we can identify, all that exists in the physical universe is imbued with and a reflection of the Divine.
- At times terrible things happen to prepare us for greater opportunities.

- Perfection ceases to be perfection if that's all there is.
- Great power in the hands of small minds is destructive.
- Don't worry about what others think. Most of the time they don't.
- A bank account reveals a person's resources but not their worth.
- Though gradual and subtle, our understanding of right and wrong changes over time.
- Only beings who have reached higher levels of consciousness can pray, "God give me more that I might have more to give. Give me less that I might have more.".
- God never impresses us to do something and then forsakes us in the doing of it.
- Nothing in creation can be understood or appreciated without a connection to that Source by which all that is has been brought into existence.
- The less conscious a person or society is, the more external controls are needed to monitor and control behavior.

- The Divine is infinitely beyond the best of our theologies and our most sacred concepts.
- Hell is not a place but a state of mind that accepts the illusion that the Creator is separate from that which he has created.
- There are no shortcuts to a relationship with the Divine.
- Anything or anyone which tries to contain or control that which was meant to be free will eventually destroy itself.
- Providence shows us the way even if we're not conscious of its guidance.
- Death is inconsistent with life. Though it continually changes form, life is all there is.
- There are times in life when the best thing we can do is nothing.
- We can learn from the past, but when the past is allowed to control, it comprises the present and casts a shadow over the future.
- Fear reacts; love responds.

- Relationships, not recognition, are the primary reason for existence.
- Though unconscious of why, for better or for worse we often choose leaders who are a reflection of ourselves.
- No matter how sophisticated, there is nothing as powerful as love.
- It's not what you have, but what has you that matters.
- When the natural is suppressed, the results are always unnatural.
- Time, a created reality, has beginnings and endings but only within the physical universe. Beyond the universe of the created, there are no beginnings and no endings for time does not exist.
- To allow the external priority over the internal compromises the purpose of existence and undermines those deeper issues which give life meaning.
- In the natural world of which we are a part, it is understood that nothing is owned, but everything is provided. Only in the land of "make-believe" inhabited by humans is ownership an accepted illusion.

- As we learn to live more fully in the moment, anxiety about the hereafter will no longer be of great concern.
- Regardless of how much they would like to share, we do not need to take on other people's dramas. We have enough of our own.
- Life is an infinitely short journey between two eternities. What we make of it is what matters.
- Whether personally or through a particular faith tradition, it is possible to become so involved in studying the God of the past that the God of the present (which is all there is) is no longer recognized.
- To honor the past and look forward to the future is fine as long as we understand the person we were yesterday and will be tomorrow is not who we are today.
- Honoring our traditions or theologies can be helpful, but if we are not aware of what's happening around us, they will not save us or our children from experiencing situations or conditions we might regret.
- There are times when we don't feel enough, but God says we are. So who has the final word?

- Love can only be experienced as it was meant to be when the human heart is transformed by the Divine.
- It is not necessarily the most beautiful flower that is the most fragrant.
- It's the struggles, the reaching out beyond ourselves that moves us to new heights and new experiences.
- We own nothing, yet everything is ours. The sooner we learn this, the "better off" we will be.
- Let me surround you with all that I am, so you might realize all that you are.
- Like a flower, love doesn't need to be noticed, just shared.
- May the sun shine to brighten your day and lighten your way.
- God reveals himself and we find ourselves in the stillness
- Forget the thorns; smell the roses!
- Expect nothing; embrace everything.
- Criticism pulls people down, but they fly on the wings of praise.

- Since when do clouds have the final word about the sun?
- We need the "rest" of God's presence.
- When you look at My face, you will see your own. When you seek my power, you will discover your own.
- Life is measured not so much on the expanse of time as it is on the eternity of the moment.
- When love is present, nothing else is needed, nor does anything else matter.
- Come close – go far.
- Theology is the study about God. Meditation is the experience of knowing God.
- Beauty that is external is temporary. Beauty that comes from within is eternal.
- Love that encourages others to be themselves is a love that is unlimited.
- Life has to do with who we know, not how well-known we are.
- Without love, life becomes an illusion and existence the only reality.

- Love is unreasonable. It doesn't need a reason to express itself.
- The heart always knows what is true even if the mind disagrees.
- Life is a process of knowing the divine and embracing the human. One cannot be experienced or understood without the other.
- Love cannot exist without expression.
- Change based on fear is destructive. Change based on love is constructive.
- Life proceeds out of what we perceive it to be. We create our own realities and then live them out.
- God's heart and God's love are as big as the universe. No one nor anything is excluded … ever.
- Where we see defects, God sees perfection.
- Like, love, beauty cannot be defined, only experienced.
- All of life has been created so we might have the opportunity of falling in love.

- When our eyes are open and we are conscious of his presence, we will understand God is never absent from us or any of his creation.
- Life often gets in the way of what we expect.
- Whether conscious or not, all relationships are built on our understanding of God and his relationship to us.
- A life lived from a place of love has no end, but goes on and on forever.
- Love needs no recognition or response. It can only be experienced and shared.
- As a glorious sunrise, beauty like love is natural. If allowed, it flows in, around, and through us.
- The purpose of life is to acquire all we can and remember all we can, so we can give all we can.
- Happiness is not only healing; it's contagious.
- There are rainbows in every cloud no matter how dark and in every drop of rain.
- Getting is never enough, but there are no limits to giving.
- Love gives us freedom to be ourselves.

- Love is the heartbeat of the universe, the vibration of the Eternal.
- Flowers fade as do our lives, but for the few moments we are here we can bring beauty to the world if we allow love to express itself through us.
- It's easy to get lost when we forget where we came from.
- Ignorance often speaks louder than the voice of reason.
- Youth has more to do with the heart and mind than the age of the forms we wear.
- Life must be lived from the inside out otherwise everything appears upside down.
- We may feel safe in our theological and philosophical towers but they will not save us if we are blind to the darkness around us.
- Over time when lies are told loud enough and long enough, the majority accept them as truth.
- Distractions come in many forms including praise and popularity.

- We warn our children about the dangers of playing with fire, yet we do the same … in ways even more dangerous.
- Everything bounded by time has a beginning and end, but that which is the Source of all … has neither.
- Consciousness and connectedness are one in the same and are the foundation and driving force behind all life in the universe.
- There are times … more or less … when less is more and more is less.

References

Light Green = Living/Facing Life

Facing Life – Moving On 9
If Only 79
Life Without Limits 117
Returning Home 143

Light Blue = Stillness/Reflection/Silence

Be Still and Know 5
And The Truth Shall Make You Free 61
In Search of Innocence 85
The Silent Treatment 87
It's Friday! 111
Time Out 114
Out of the Silence 135

Light Yellow = Time/Life's Timeline

What Time Is It? 13
Who Am I? 27
As The Years Go By 36
Treasures in Time 80
A Journey Through Time 95
Ageless Solutions For A Better Tomorrow 150

Light Orange/Peach = The World Today & Holidays/Special Section

Never Forgotten 16
What in the World's Going On? 155
Christmas – A Time to Remember 165
Holiday Memories 167
The Spirit of the Season 170
Christmas – A Time for Embracing The "Present" 172
To Broadway With Love 174
A New Beginning 176
A Cry of Innocence 178

Soft Lime Green = Relationships/Team

You Own What? 23
Who Says I Have to Be Right 51
Being A Part of the Team 57
The Road to Success 64
Face to Face 74
Life is For-giving, Not For-getting 76
A Word to The Wise 96
The Journey 99
Standing Together 110
A Composition of the Ages 137

Grey = Self

From The External to the Internal 17
Beauty or the Beast 38
Everyday Heroes 55
Reflections or Reality 139

Lilac = Faith/God/Spirit

Concepts For Living 30
Now You See Him – Now You Don't 40
The Spirit of Who We Are 106

Aqua = Who We Are

To Be or Not to Be 58
So How Do We Measure Up? 82
Possibilities Unlimited 91
Imperfectly Perfect 120
The Ideal and the Real 127

Violet = Child

On The Other Side of Reason 19
The Child Within 21
A Celebration in Time 53
On Becoming a Child 93
The Awakening 102
Happiness is … 118

Light Pink = Challenges/Challenging Time

Distracted 11
The Me That I Am 59
Darkness May Come, But So Does the Dawn 63
Common Ground 66
Detours 90
Accepting the Unacceptable 101
Hope 104
Commitment 108
The Shadow Side of the Beautiful 109
Seeing is Believing, Or Is It? 115
The Challenge of Change 126
Your Attention Please 141

Berry = Gratefulness

The Sound of Music 7
The Gift 26
The "Present" 50
The Best Gifts in Life Are Free 149

Rose = Love

A Force of Nature 32
Love 113
Another Look at Love 125

Credits

Image by <a href="https://www.freepik.com/free-vector/hand-drawn-tree-life-brownshades_10502870.htm#query=tree%20outline&position=2&from_view=keyword&track=ais">Freepik</a>

Page i

Image by <a href="https://www.freepik.com/free-vector/beautiful-vintage-vector-decorative-elements-ornaments_10700742.htm#query=scroll&position=41&from_view=search&track=sph">Image by macrovector</a> on Freepik

Page 29

https://www.swagroup.com/projects/the-clearing-sandy-hook-permanent-memorial/(Copyright 2023 SWA Group)

Page 181

https://www.dreamstime.com/ (licensed)

Made in the USA
Columbia, SC
30 November 2024